MORRIS AUTOMATED INFORMATION NETWORK

0 1006 0102990 1

JUL 21 1999

Chester
Library

DISCARD

250 West Main Street
Chester, NJ 07930

P9-EGK-172

ON-LINE

CHESTER LIBRARY
CHESTER, NJ 07930

DEMCO

Plants for All Seasons

Plants for All Seasons

Beautiful and versatile plants that change through the year

URSULA BUCHAN

PHOTOGRAPHS BY HOWARD RICE

MITCHELL BEAZLEY

I should like to thank my husband, Charles Wide,
for his encouragement and support during the writing of this book

PLANTS FOR ALL SEASONS

First published in Great Britain in 1999 by Mitchell Beazley,
an imprint of Octopus Publishing Group Ltd,
Michelin House, 81 Fulham Road,
London SW3 6RB

Text copyright © Ursula Buchan 1999
Copyright © Octopus Publishing Group Ltd 1999

All rights reserved.
No part of this work may be reproduced or utilized in any
form or by any means, electronic or mechanical, including
photocopying, recording or by any information storage
and retrieval system, without the prior written
permission of the publisher

ISBN 1-84000-051-1

A CIP catalogue copy of this book is available
from the British Library

Executive Editor: **Alison Starling**
Executive Art Editor: **Vivienne Brar**
Senior Editor: **Michèle Byam**
Designer: **Martin Bristow**
Production: **Rachel Staveley**
Picture Research: **Jenny Faithfull**
Indexer: **Ann Barrett**

Set in Guardi

Printed and bound in China by
Toppan Printing Co., (H.K.) Ltd.

CONTENTS

the joy of multiseasonal plants

esponse to the seasons is very deeply embedded in our psyches. Instinctively, we react positively to seeing the first snowdrop, not merely because of its beauty, but because it heralds the awakening of our garden from winter's 'sleep'. Today, although we are less seasonally aware than in the past – we can now enjoy strawberries in winter and tangerines in summer – nothing can quite smother the profound sense of anticipation that we feel at the onset of each new season.

We are inclined to take the seasonal development of plants in our garden for granted. We know that they grow and mature, come into leaf, then flower, fruit, and decay, yet it is rare for us to reflect on how this process works. The aim of this book is to encourage you, the reader, to look more closely at plants, and to show how, with enhanced awareness of seasonal changes, you can get the best out of your garden.

For many people, the planting of a garden consists of taking a trip to a garden centre on the first fine day of spring and picking out a variety of plants in pots, usually those which, by a happy accident, are in flower. Rarely is there much information on the container's label describing how the plant develops and changes through the year, and a

BELOW *Chaenomeles* x *superba* is an example of a plant which only shows its full potential as a multiseasonal plant when established in the garden.

photograph will only usually show the plant at one particular moment of its development. As a result, the impulsive plant-buyer can end up with a garden heavily weighted towards spring-flowerers, and with little else of interest for the rest of the year.

The plants are then taken home and planted where they will associate well with others in flower. However, as the season wears on, the gardener may be taken quite by surprise: the plants change – slowly and subtly but irrevocably – as does the relationship between the plants in a group. Unlike the still-attached colourful labels, which have remained resolutely the same, the plants themselves are now very different.

This point may be illustrated by reference to a small tree, the paper birch (*Betula papyrifera*). The label extols the virtues of the plant's peeling chalk-white bark, so the gardener may well decide to plant *Berberis* 'Rose Glow' near its base, fancying the sight of the white, glistening bark rising above a dome of pink, purple, and cream-variegated leaves. What he or she may not have bargained for is that the leaves of the berberis will turn from bluish pink variegations in summer to deep scarlet red tints by mid-autumn. At the same time, the

leaves of the birch will have been transformed from their dark summer green to a delicate, but winning, butter-yellow. Fortunately, this is also an attractive colour combination, but it is entirely fortuitous. Yet, if gardeners had a better idea originally of how plants change during the course of the year, how much more often could they paint these attractive garden pictures.

Not all plants undergo such distinct transformations. Evergreens often appear unchanging, although on close inspection it becomes apparent that they do not remain exactly the same throughout the year (*see p.17*). Of course, we do need some plants that we can depend on to remain more or less constant: a yew hedge (*Taxus*) may change subtly in the spring, when the light-green young growth appears, but it is, fundamentally, an important provider of immutable shelter and background for colourful flowers.

When planning a garden, consider carefully your choice of plants before you make any firm decisions: plants that most clearly exhibit seasonal features are usually garden-worthy, and especially those that are multiseasonal, performing for more than one season of the year. Multiseasonal plants are particularly vital in a small garden, where you need to make the best and most fruitful use of limited space. This book concentrates on plants that genuinely provide substantial and varying interest throughout two seasons or occasionally more; indeed, a small number of plants, such as some birches and maples, have something to offer the observer on every day of the year. All too often we neglect our gardens over winter, but in our increasingly pressurized lives, a garden has an important part to play in spiritual and physical refreshment all year round, and not just in the growing months.

Observing the transformation of a plant at close quarters is tremendously enjoyable, but it is all the more rewarding if you know what to look for. The first section of the book, 'Nature in Transformation', examines the changes that take place in plants throughout the seasons: the way that leaves emerge, mature and decay; the transformation of flowers to berries or seedheads; the beauty of bark and stems, and their importance in enhancing the garden scene, especially in winter; and the impact that the habit and form of a plant have on the garden at different times of year.

The second half of the book, 'Plants for all Seasons', is devoted to non-botanical descriptions of some of the best multiseasonal plants, together with short notes on their use. For convenience, I have divided it into the main plant groups: shrubs; climbers and wall shrubs; border plants; and trees, although these are artificial divisions, of course (for example, woody plants are often planted in borders).

ABOVE *Berberis* 'Rose Glow' in summer, showing the variegation on the young leaves.
RIGHT The sometimes exceptional beauty of stems in winter is exemplified by this *Cornus sanguinea* 'Winter Beauty'.

The plants are listed alphabetically by botanical name within each section. The fact that common names can differ from one country, or even one county, to another makes their use impracticable. In the glossary at the end of the book, I have tried to include many of the 'Latin' names of species mentioned and their meanings in the hope that this will add to your enjoyment, or at least diminish confusion.

Each plant entry includes the height and spread of the plant, but bear in mind that soil, aspect, climate, and origin affect the size of plants, so those quoted can only ever be very approximate. The heights and spreads cited are ultimate, which means that, particularly in the case of trees and shrubs, they may not be attained for many years. Information on cultivation, in all its aspects, is only provided as a guide. Much of successful gardening is a matter of trial and error, for plants are subject to all the vagaries of living things. Moreover each garden is individual. On the subject of propagation, it must be understood that, although many plants can be successfully propagated by amateur gardeners, there are some techniques, in particular grafting, which are really the province of commercial growers.

LEFT *Papaver somniferum* shows very clearly how different a plant can look in flower and seed.
BELOW A well-planted garden in summer, with an attractive mixture of flowers, seedheads, foliage and interesting plant habits.

Some plant families are more multiseasonal than others, and are thus heavily represented. The rose family (*Rosaceae*), which includes *Cotoneaster*, *Malus*, *Pyrus* and *Sorbus*, is the richest. Fortunately, many of these do well even in small gardens.

Although the book is heavily weighted in favour of plants that are suitable for a small garden, some larger specimens have found a place. Not many people have room for the fine tulip tree, *Liriodendron tulipifera*, for example, but it would be a pity not to recognize it when you see it.

We owe it to ourselves to get the most from our garden plants. However, I would never suggest that a garden should contain exclusively multiseasonal plants: if there are no plants with fugitive flowers, or fleeting charm, there will be a kind of predictability about the garden scene. Sometimes it is justified to let an area of the garden go quiet for a time.

Plenty of widely available garden plants offer seasonal variety, and there are numerous excellent examples that I have not been able to include here. I fervently hope that this book will inspire you to embark on a voyage of discovery – to seek out, experiment with, and above all enjoy your own 'plants for all seasons'.

ABOVE As an annual, *Nicandra physalodes* must flower and seed in the course of a few months.
RIGHT *Sedum spectabile* is a plant with both long-lasting flowers and a striking habit.

nature in transformation

FOLIAGE AND TEXTURE

Foliage, both deciduous and evergreen, plays a central and sometimes colourful part on the garden stage; often in its own right or as a foil and background for flowers. Many change in aspect in the course of the season, altering the garden picture picture as they do so.

There was a time in my life (and perhaps in yours as well?) when – in as much as I thought about the subject at all – I was inclined to dismiss the foliage of garden plants as 'just leaves'. Flowers were what gardens were really about, as far as I was concerned. Until I became positively interested in gardening, and began really looking at plants, I did not fully appreciate the central role that foliage plays on the garden stage.

For most, if not all, deciduous plants, their appearance is influenced greatly by the presence, or absence, of leaves. A bare tree, say an ornamental spindle tree like *Euonymus alatus*, presents a markedly different aspect depending on the time of year. In winter, we are aware of the corky, winged bark of the trunk and stems, the shape of the crown, and the dense, zig-zag branches, but in spring and particularly autumn, these attributes are masked by the leaves and, to some extent, by colourful fruits.

Foliage dictates the aspect of many plants, both deciduous and evergreen, however much emphasis we put on flowers. For flowers, on many plants, are very short-lived. An attractive and garden-worthy plant, such as the Caucasian peony (*Paeonia mlokosewitschii*), will carry flowers for only two to four weeks in the year, in late spring or very early summer. If the weather is wet at this time, the flowers may be spoiled, and the gardener will have to be philosophical about the loss and wait for another year. The sculptural, bluish green foliage, on the

ABOVE, LEFT TO RIGHT **The young toothed leaves of the grape vine, *Vitis vinifera* 'Purpurea', are grey and intensely hairy; but gradually the hairs drop, and the mature leaf is matt and deep purple.**
OPPOSITE **In autumn, the leaves turn glowing crimson before they fall.**

other hand, adds interest to the border from spring until late autumn, changing colour until it eventually falls. With the katsura tree (*Cercidiphyllum japonicum*), the flowers scarcely feature at all; they are tiny, short-lived, and borne before the leaves appear. It is the gorgeous leaf colour (bronze in spring, red and yellow in autumn) that is the glory of this tree.

The fascination of leaves lies as much in their mutability as in their variety. The average leaf will change enormously in the course of the season, sometimes altering beyond recognition the look of a plant. Deciduous leaves unfurl slowly in spring, gradually elongating as the days go by. This process in itself can be very pleasurable to watch, especially in the case of *Cotoneaster horizontalis*, whose leaves emerge folded before they open out, or the holly (*Ilex aquifolium* 'Argentea Marginata'), whose young foliage is tinged purple. Particularly enjoyable to observe is the way that the ultimately huge leaves of *Darmera peltata* grow up and out as they expand in spring.

The eventual leaf size obviously depends on the plant type, but may also be influenced by position, soil, and climate, so that it may not be quite the same from one year to the next. There are also usually variations in size between leaves on the same plant.

Some leaves open out very quickly, others may show their undersides prominently at first. This is certainly the case of the whitebeam (*Sorbus aria*). The silver-haired

young leaves grow almost vertically initially, giving the tree the look, from a distance, of a stunning flowering magnolia. The hairs gradually drop off, so that the mature leaf shows more clearly its essential nature, which is smooth and dark green on the upper side and silver beneath.

There are a good number of plants that have spring tints to their leaves, a fact that is often overlooked. However, it is the major selling point of the ornamental crab apple, *Malus* x *purpurea* 'Eleyi', for example. The young leaves are a purple-bronze when they first unfurl, as are the young shoots. Gradually, as spring advances, the leaves become purple-green. The lovely flowers, good fruit, and excellent autumn leaf colour are all added bonuses.

One of my other favourites for the same reason is the ornamental vine *Vitis vinifera* 'Purpurea'. Like the whitebeam, it has silver hairs that thickly cover the very young leaves, partially obscuring the purple ground colour beneath. This silvery purple foliage associates very well with climbers with blue flowers, such as *Clematis macropetala* and the large-flowered *C.* 'Perle d'Azur'.

Other plants with leaves that change colour in late spring or summer include *Amelanchier lamarckii* (from hairy and bronze to hairless and dark green), *Artemisia lactiflora* 'Guizhou' (from purple to green), *Catalpa bignonioides* 'Aurea' (from bronze to bright yellow), and *Epimedium* x *rubrum* (from coral-red to green). Trees with yellow or bronze spring foliage are particularly desirable, and look splendid underplanted with pale yellow daffodils.

The mature leaf also undergoes changes. The foliage of many deciduous trees gradually turns a darker colour as the season wears on so that, by late summer, it has lost its springtime freshness but has gained considerably in sober depth. This feature is particularly evident in whitebeams (*Sorbus aria*) and apples (*Malus*), both ornamental and edible. Indeed, gardeners make a point of waiting until the leaves of apple and pear trees go dark green before they consider it time to 'summer prune' them.

It is in autumn, however, that the changing nature of foliage is most striking. Since food is no longer manufactured in the leaf, its colour changes once more. The green chlorophyll in the cells deteriorates, leaving the more persistent anthocyanins and carotene to show up clearly. These give the leaf a red, yellow, or brown appearance, or sometimes a mixture of colours. Gradually, as all the food is withdrawn from the leaf, an 'abscission layer' grows between stem and leaf stalk and, once the leaf is completely separated internally from the stem, it is ready to fall. This process is accelerated by high winds or frosts. In the case of whitebeams, the heavy leaves will sometimes silver the ground beneath the tree for weeks, until finally blown away.

LEFT **The broadly arching leaves of the zebra grass,** *Miscanthus sinensis* **'Zebrinus', go yellow in autumn, masking somewhat the vivid white or pale yellow summer stripes.**

Before they fall, the leaves of many deciduous plants often shrink or curl, which can change the appearance of a plant altogether. A shrub that seems dense and well clothed in summer can become lighter and airier, with the structure of the plant more obvious as leaf-fall approaches. The bones, as it were, become visible beneath the skin.

The colour and reliability of autumn tints are potent indicators of a worthwhile garden plant. However, reliability is not universal, since the intensity, and even the tint, are affected by the climate, so that it can vary considerably from one geographical region to another, and from one year to the next. Factors such as hours of sunshine during the summer, and temperatures in the autumn, both make a difference. Although no plant can be guaranteed to offer spectacular autumn colour year after year, the most dependable (in the plant directory) are maples (*Acer*), amelanchiers, berberis, birches (*Betula*), dogwoods (*Cornus*), deciduous cotoneasters, the cockspur hawthorn (*Crataegus persimilis* 'Prunifolia'), the winged spindle (*Euonymus alatus*), *Fothergilla major* 'Monticola', *Geranium macrorrhizum*, witch hazels (*Hamamelis*), the climbing hydrangea (*Hydrangea anomala* subsp. *petiolaris*), apples (*Malus*), Chinese Virginia creeper (*Parthenocissus henryana*), *Rhododendron luteum*,

ABOVE LEFT **The leaves of *Catalpa bignonioides* 'Aurea' go from bronze to yellow and, finally, lime-green.** ABOVE RIGHT **No leaf of *Cyclamen hederifolium* is identical to another.**

hedgehog rose (*Rosa rugosa*), deciduous viburnums, the rowan (*Sorbus commixta* 'Embley'), and the grape vine (*Vitis vinifera* 'Purpurea').

Knowledge of the usual autumn tints of a plant can, and indeed should, influence the decision as to where to place it in the garden. For example, a climbing plant such as the Chinese Virginia creeper (*Parthenocissus henryana*) or *Vitis vinifera* 'Purpurea' will look stunning against a yellow brick or stone wall, but will clash with one of bright red brick. When planting a group of shrubs, it is just as important to consider how the foliage might look together in autumn as it is to consider how the plants might associate in flower.

Although often less obvious, changes also occur to evergreen foliage in the course of a year. Their mutability can be seen very clearly in a golden conifer, whose bright colour in spring may dull as the summer goes on; or in a heath like *Calluna vulgaris* 'Robert Chapman' (golden in summer; orange-red in winter); or in the common holly *Ilex aquifolium* 'Argentea Marginata', which has purple-flushed leaves when young. Alternatively, the changes can be more subtle, as when the fresh new leaves of Portugal laurel (*Prunus lusitanica*) or bergenias emerge among the older ones. Bergenias, such as *B.* 'Sunningdale' and *B.* 'Abendglut', have leaves that take on a purple or red colour as temperatures drop in autumn; the same happens to the semi-evergreen *Geranium macrorrhizum*, as well as the evergreen, variegated *Euonymus fortunei* cultivars such as 'Emerald 'n' Gold' and 'Emerald Gaiety'.

Another winning feature of foliage is the almost infinite range of individual leaf shapes. Leaves are broadly described as either simple, with a continuous surface, or compound, when the leaf is made up of several leaflets. However, within these two categories there are numerous variations. Among the simple leaves are the delicate 'fingers' of the Japanese maple (such as *Acer palmatum* 'Sango-kaku'), the enormous hearts of the Indian bean tree (*Catalpa bignonioides*), the thin grass-blades of *Helictotrichon sempervirens*, and the jagged, spiny leaves of the common holly (*Ilex aquifolium*). Compound leaves include those of the Hubei rowan (*Sorbus hupehensis*), the three-lobed shamrock of the paper-bark maple (*Acer griseum*), and the finely pinnate fronds of the shuttlecock fern (*Matteuccia struthiopteris*).

The shape of individual leaves affects the overall look of the plant, as does the arrangement of leaves on the shoots. The effect created by the many tiny, thick-cuticled, densely spaced leaves of the checkerberry or wintergreen (*Gaultheria procumbens*), for example, is rather different from that of an airier plant such as barrenwort (*Epimedium* x *versicolor* 'Sulphureum'). They are

both groundcover plants that thrive in shady places, but the former creates a darker, more sombre atmosphere than the latter. They are not interchangeable plants just because they like the same conditions. Similarly, a silver birch, such as *Betula pendula* 'Laciniata', will make a very different impression on the garden scene from a young tulip tree (*Liriodendron tulipifera*). The birch, with its very light, widely spaced leaves, can be looked through, even in high summer, whereas the large, simple leaves of the tulip tree form a dense growth that creates an almost solid obstacle to the eye.

Foliage is a crucial feature of any well-planned planting scheme, and can create a tremendous impact. Stark contrasts in leaf are often far more tolerable to the eye than strong contrasts in flower colour; the fact that most foliage is green – even though there are innumerable shades of green – means that the eye will settle happily on the differences in shape, and be satisfied and stimulated by them.

We should also appreciate the immense variety of leaf textures. The hard, glistening leaves of hollies have the effect of drawing the eye more, say, than the soft, delicate foliage of a birch. Interesting and satisfying combinations of plants can be achieved just by contrasting leaf texture. A successful waterside planting, for example, might combine the soft, vertical fronds of shuttlecock ferns (*Matteuccia struthiopteris*) with the deeply veined, leathery, palm-like foliage of *Rodgersia*

BELOW **The leaves of the birch *Betula papyifera* take on lovely orange-yellow tones as autumn progresses.**

aesculifolia or the smooth, light-reflecting leaves of *Darmera peltata*. The tactile nature of some foliage also adds to our appreciation: few people can walk past lamb's ears (*Stachys byzantina*) on a summer's day without the urge to touch their furry leaves.

Even in the depths of winter, foliage has a part to play. Clearly, evergreens dominate the garden scene, but there is also a selection of deciduous plants that persist over winter, even if in a different form. The leaves of grasses – *Deschampsia*, *Festuca*, *Helictotrichon*, *Miscanthus*, *Pennisetum*, and *Stipa*, for example – may have lost their colour by the end of autumn, but they will persist until the spring, when fresh growths burst forth to mask them.

Remember also that there are a few deciduous plants that die down in summer and grow in winter, rather than the other way round. This is the result of climatic conditions in their native habitats, but it is a very useful attribute which gardeners can use. *Cyclamen hederifolium* and *Eranthis hyemalis* are two such plants, and are immensely valuable: their absence in summer goes without remark, but their presence in winter is a great cause for celebration.

ABOVE ***Fothergilla major*** can be relied upon for
the rich warmth of its autumn colour.
RIGHT **Even evergreens can turn colour at certain
times of the year. Here, a *Mahonia japonica*
displays a wide range of tints in early winter.**

FLOWERS TO SEEDHEADS

The gradual transformation in plants from flowering to fruiting can change the
face of a garden as much even as the 'leafing-up' of trees and shrubs in spring.
We can use this progression to our advantage when designing our gardens,
to give interest and variety through the growing season.

When they first begin a garden, the majority of people concentrate their interest and energies on flowers. This is quite understandable. Familiar and generally colourful, flowers will always be immensely important to gardeners. But there is much more to the business of garden making than simply cultivating flowers, even if they provide the best starting point.

The variety of flower forms in nature is breathtakingly large: from the two-lipped trumpets of snapdragons to the curved 'keels' of sweet peas; from the small tubes of buddleja to the open cups of apple blossom; and from bell-shaped clematis to pendent catkins of birch. The forms can be homely and familiar, like the flat heads of cow parsley flowers, or strange and exotic, like the conical flowers of the tulip tree (*Liriodendron tulipifera*).

What is likely to strike the casual observer just as strongly, however, is the enormous range of colour in flowers, from snow-white to deepest purple and everything in between, not to mention 'bi-colours' and multi-coloured flowers. The colour may be pure, or it may come in stripes, blotches, or spots. This is surely the reason why so many people begin their gardening careers with an interest in roses – this genus includes every colour except blue (and that colour cannot be too far away!). There is also the scent of flowers – an aspect that becomes increasingly important to gardeners the more time they spend in the garden.

ABOVE, LEFT TO RIGHT **A close-up of the flowers of *Crataegus persimilis* 'Prunifolia' (syn. *C. crus-galli*); the same plant taken just as the berries begin to redden in early autumn; later in the autumn when the leaves have taken on rich tints.**
OPPOSITE ***Crataegus persimilis* 'Prunifolia' is a small or medium-sized tree with a rounded shape; it is suitable for growing as a specimen or for closing a vista.**

What may not be immediately obvious is that flowers alter through the flowering season. To begin with, a flower's colour can vary. The flowers of the rose 'Peace', for example, are yellow at first, but gradually acquire pink and red tones; the flowers of *Cornus* 'Norman Hadden' begin snow-white, but gradually turn to pink. For these plants, changing colour is an inevitable part of the ageing process. For others, it is prompted by lower temperatures; many white roses – 'Iceberg', for example – will take on pink tinges as autumn progresses and the nights gradually become colder.

Flowering can be manipulated in a number of ways by the gardener. Altering the timing of flowering by the use of artificial lighting is a technique for the greenhouse and not in the province of this book, but outside there is much that can be done – by disbudding and 'stopping' – to alter both the size of flower and the flowering period. With annuals the timing of flowering can be affected by the sowing date. In some plant genera, the removal of the first flush of blooms will stimulate plants to produce a second crop of flowers. Many types of roses will flower more than once, even if they are not scrupulously deadheaded (although that helps), but herbaceous geraniums, for example, need encouraging by the removal of the first flowers once they have faded. This kind of intervention risks the quantity and quality of berries or seedheads because it delays, or even stops, the forming of

fruit. However, in some cases – especially herbaceous geraniums or dianthus that don't bear conspicuous fruit in any event – the benefits outweigh the disadvantages.

Flowers are immensely alluring in terms of scent, shape, and colour, and it is tempting to fill the garden with them; however, we must remember that they can be disappointingly short-lived. The individual flowers of morning glory (*Ipomoea*) and daylilies (*Hemerocallis*) last for less than a day, although they bloom in succession over several weeks, and the flowering period of many ornamental cherries lasts little more than two weeks. The number of genera that flower for more than one month are decidedly limited, and are much prized if they do. Anthemis, argyranthemums, penstemons, potentillas, viburnums, and chrysanthemums, as well as hardy and half-hardy annuals, are all relatively long-flowering, but generally we must assume a few weeks' flowering at the most, unless climatic conditions, or an absence of pollinators, are particularly favourable to longevity.

It therefore makes good sense to find space for plants that do not necessarily have showy flowers, even in a small garden, provided that they have some other marked characteristic, such as wonderful foliage or attractive fruit. Generally, in the case of trees, and sometimes in the case even of shrubs, features other than flowers must appeal to the gardener. *Callicarpa bodinieri* var. *giraldii* 'Profusion', for example, makes up for its lack of conspicuous flowers in striking fruit, as does *Gaultheria procumbens*.

Of course, there are some exceptional trees and shrubs – *Malus* and *Sorbus*, as well as other plants in the rose (*Rosaceae*) family – that have both lovely blossom and handsome fruit in sufficient quantity to strike the eye at a distance, and so earn their keep twice over. When you consider that many of these also have marvellous autumn foliage colour, it is not surprising that they are usually the first choice for all but the tiniest gardens.

An especially versatile performer is the Fuji cherry (*Prunus incisa*). The white or pale pink, saucer-shaped flowers appear before the leaves in early spring, and are produced in profusion, either singly or in small clusters. They are occasionally followed by small, oval, deep purple fruits . The green leaves are ovate and toothed, and bronze-coloured when they emerge; in autumn, they take on lovely flame tints before they fall.

The Fuji cherry is amenable to being grown either as a large, spreading shrub or as a small, rounded tree; it is therefore suitable for any size of garden. But it can also be planted in a line, and annually trimmed, to make an unusual

ABOVE *Staphylea colchica* is grown for its fragrant flowers in late spring, and strange, bladder-like fruits in late summer.
LEFT The white or pale pink flowers of the Fuji cherry, *Prunus incisa*, appear before the leaves in early and mid-spring.

flowering hedge. In its native Japan, it has long been a popular subject for bonsai treatment (that is, grown in an ornamental pot with the roots regularly clipped to dwarf its growth). Because it flowers in very early spring (and there are even earlier named cultivars, such as *P.i.* 'February Pink' and *P.i.* 'Praecox'), it associates well with early-flowering narcissi and other bulbs, and creates an impact before the majority of garden flowers really hit their stride. I am not sure that you could expect more of a garden plant than all of that.

Much as we might like to believe otherwise, plants do not flower entirely for our benefit, but in order to attract suitable pollinators. The task of pollinators is to fertilize the ovules at the base of each flower so that they develop viable seed to perpetuate the species. The seed is often protected by an outer covering until the moment comes for it to be released, to germinate, and then produce new plants. We rather loosely call these coverings 'fruits'.

Fruits, berries and seed capsules offer an infinite variety of colours and shapes to enrich our gardens. Many are fleshy, like strawberries, pears or apples (small soft fruits are often referred to as berries); others are dry and hard, like those of

RIGHT The snake-bark maple, *Acer capillipes*, does not have very showy flowers, but the fruit make a strong impact.
BELOW Each daylily (*Hemerocallis* 'Hyperion') flower lasts only a day, but there is a succession. The hollyhocks (*Alcea rugosa*) also flower in succession.

maple (*Acer*) or hazelnuts (*Corylus*). Some, such as those of the shrub, commonly known as the bladdernut, *Staphylea colchica* are even bladder-like, inflating as they ripen.

Seeds are dispersed in many ways. Some enfolded in edible fruits and berries, are scattered by humans or, even more often, by birds and small mammals. Inedible fruits float, spin or simply drop to the ground, are caught on the fur of animals or are blown by the wind.

Observing the gradual transition from flower to fruit is one of the great attractions of having a garden, but it requires patience. In most cases, it occurs stealthily. First the flower buds appear; these slowly elongate until they burst, causing the petals to unfold and expand. The flowers are then at their best for a few hours, days, or weeks, before the petals drop, revealing a small – in some cases scarcely discernible – immature fruit. This fruit will grow, deepen in colour, and mature, until it eventually falls to the ground. It is this slow metamorphosis that allows the gardener so much scope in creating different scenes and effects in the garden.

We can see the process of flower to fruit very clearly in a plant such as *Hypericum* x *inodorum* 'Elstead'. In early- and midsummer, this smallish, deciduous or sometimes semi-

ABOVE **The transformation that takes place with *Viburnum opulus* 'Xanthocarpum', from flat 'lacecap hydrangea' type flowers to ovoid, orange berries is a pleasure to watch.**

evergreen shrub is covered in clusters of yellow, saucer-like flowers with distinctive bristles of protruding stamens. The flowers are clean and bright, and contrast pleasingly with the dark green, oval leaves. As the summer wears on, and the pollinators get to work, the fertilized ovaries of some of these flowers slowly develop into ovoid fruit, first whitish pink in colour, then darkening to a bright orange-red. This plant is unusual, although not unique, in that you will find fruit and flowers on the same truss, producing a most unusual and distinctive colour combination, which can be happily included in any late summer bronze or yellow colour scheme.

The changes are more subtle in an apple tree, but are nevertheless apparent with careful observation. The petals drop, the ovary expands, is ovoid at first, then becomes progressively rounder as the fruit develops. The fruitlet is green initially, turning red and yellow just before the fruit is ready to drop in autumn. Some cultivars remain green; indeed their colour is one way of identifying a particular variety. As the fruit gains in size, the whole appearance of the tree can change: the branches may become more horizontal, even pendulous, under the increasing weight.

In some cases the changes take place quite quickly, especially in annual plants, which complete their life-cycle in a single growing season. The opium poppy (*Papaver somniferum*) is a particular source of wonder to the gardener, since it undergoes a substantial transformation in only five months. In spring, the seed will germinate in a fortnight, and the leaves and the 60cm- (24in-) tall stem grow in as little as six to eight weeks. In midsummer, the first flowers burst out of their round buds. The petals then fall and the seed capsules expand so that by early autumn, what was so recently a confection of tissue-paper petals is now a sturdy, flat-headed pepper-pot full of seeds. Often these seed capsules are cut off to prevent prodigious seeding, or are removed for winter decoration in the house.

In *Catalpa bignonioides*, the transformation of large, upright, foxglove-type flowers into long, stringy, pendulous black beans is remarkable. Almost as spectacular is the change that takes place in *Clematis tangutica*: from yellow, leathery, bell-shaped flowers to fluffy, round, silken seedheads.

The knowledge that plants change, often dramatically, in the course of a season, gives us the chance to create some striking effects in the garden that could not be achieved with

RIGHT The flowers of *Cornus* 'Eddie's White Wonder' (here in spring) begin cup-shaped and then open out. They start with a pinky edge, then turn pure white, before acquiring pink tints as they fade.
BELOW There is a stark beauty to the seedheads of *Miscanthus sinensis* and (behind) *Achillea filipendulina* in early winter.

flowering plants alone. For example, berrying plants, which produce yellow, orange, or scarlet fruit when ripe, combine magnificently with plants with deciduous leaves that acquire similar tints in autumn. Autumn-flowering plants, such as garden chrysanthemums, are also similar in colour, so combine harmoniously with autumn berries and foliage.

For striking colour contrasts, choose berrying evergreen plants. *Gaultheria procumbens* and *Skimmia japonica* are both glossy-leaved evergreens, with contrasting bright berries, that make an excellent weed-suppressing carpet beneath established paperbark maples (*Acer griseum*) or birches (*Betula*) in gardens with acid soil. In winter, when the trees' leaves have fallen and the berries have been eaten by birds or

LEFT **The delicate summer flowers of *Gaultheria procumbens*, a groundcover woodland plant, are followed by bright red berries.**
BELOW **Summer flowers are supplemented, where gaps have been left by spring flowering bulbs, by half-hardy annuals, like yellow *Tagetes* at the front.**
OPPOSITE **The florets of *Echinops ritro* open from the top downwards over several days.**

have decayed, there is a different but also pleasing picture composed of neat, glossy green foliage beneath cinnamon-barked maples and stark white-barked birches.

If you are growing plants for their berries, consider those whose fruits are particularly long-lasting. There is substantial variation in this respect between genera – the fruit of the Fuji cherry (*Prunus incisa*), for example, will be eaten long before those of the crab apple, *Malus* 'Golden Hornet' – and even between different cultivars or species within a genus. This is often related to their attractiveness to birds, and may differ from season to season, depending on the availability of other food sources.

Another factor to consider is the susceptibility of some fruit to disease. For example, all pyracanthas have attractive fruit, but some are plagued by a disfiguring fungus called pyracantha scab. It makes sense to choose a cultivated variety, such as *P.* 'Navaho', which has been selected because of its resistance to this fungus.

Not all fruits are, in themselves, attractive or distinctive. Many are easily passed over, until the morning after a sharp frost, perhaps, when a drab plant will suddenly take centre stage, the glistening rime in the sunshine outlining a previously unnoticed sculptural shape: achilleas, *Dictamnus albus* var. *purpureus*, and *Echinops ritro* are good examples. Others have immediately striking seedheads, particularly *Sedum* 'Herbstfreude', any evergreen grass such as *Miscanthus* or *Helictotrichon*, and the sea holly (*Eryngium bourgatii*).

The attractiveness of seedheads should affect the timetable of gardening work. It makes little sense to cut every seeding herbaceous perennial down to their crowns in autumn, if you thereby deny some plants of one last chance to shine.

True gardeners appreciate the end of the plant's natural cycle of growth just as much as the beginning, and are never too anxious to snuff out a lingering life. Dying plants, or parts of plants, often have a beauty and dignity of their own. The dried yellow foliage of grasses, the hollow capsules of poppies crackling with dislodged poppy seeds, and the dinner-plate heads of achillea all enhance the garden in early winter. How plants die is enormously influenced by climatic factors. Some years, it will be a wash-out (literally because of heavy rain), while in warm, sunny autumns and cold but dry winters, plants continue to give value for many weeks. If possible, some plants should be left to die gracefully, not cut off prematurely before they are ready to take their leave.

OPPOSITE **The bead-like clusters of berries of** *Callicarpa* x *bodinieri* var. *giraldii* **'Profusion' are carried in autumn.**
ABOVE AND RIGHT **'Scabrosa' is a particularly good form of** *Rosa rugosa*, **with large flowers and glossy, dark-green foliage. This rose should never be deadheaded because of its longlasting spherical hips.**

BARK AND STEMS

There is much more emphasis on the virtues of bark and stems these days, but there is still some way to go before they are accepted as central to the desirablility of planting certain species of trees and shrubs, if gardens are to be places of interest and refuge in winter time.

The wonderful potential of textured bark and coloured stems is often overlooked by gardeners. This is not entirely surprising, since an appreciation is likely to develop only after the possibilities of flowers and leaves have been fully explored. It is heartening that commentators now lay much more emphasis on the virtues of bark, but there is still some way to go before gardeners themselves accept it as central to the desirability of trees and shrubs, if gardens are to be places of interest and refuge in winter.

Bark is, by its very nature, changeable. It usually becomes thicker as the plant gets older. However, in some genera (*Betula*, *Eucalyptus*, *Platanus*, *Prunus*, and one *Acer*) the outer layer tends to peel away from time to time to reveal fresh new, steel-smooth wood underneath. In the case of the London plane (*Platanus orientalis*), this sloughing of parts of the bark has the effect of limiting air pollution damage to the plant, hence the popularity of this tree in towns and cities.

Some of the most ornamental examples of bark-sloughing can be found among Asian or North American forms of birch, such as *Betula papyrifera* and *B. alleghaniensis*. Observing the process is as fascinating and rewarding as watching a snake slough a skin. This peeling does not happen all over the tree trunk at the same time, so several colours can be present simultaneously. In some birch species, the bark curls back like wood shavings, in others it

ABOVE, LEFT AND RIGHT **In the first photograph, the form of the white willow, *Salix alba* subsp. *vitellina* 'Britzensis', is seen in late spring, two months after the branches have been cut close to the main trunk. This is called pollarding. The next photograph was taken a few weeks later, when shoots were growing quickly.**
OPPOSITE **The leaves are shown turning in late autumn, whilst below the stems can be seen in their full winter glory.**

hangs in rags and tatters from the branches (this happens also with *Acer griseum*). It may peel in diagonal or horizontal stripes. The barks of ornamental cherries (*Prunus*) also often peel horizontally.

Because birch bark is so thin, the breathing pores (lenticels) are very obvious; they can also be ornamental, appearing often as striking horizontal lines on the bark. The white, peeling bark of the canoe or paper birch, *Betula papyrifera*, is sufficiently absorbent to take ink, so can be used as writing paper, an attribute that fascinates anyone fortunate enough to see it done. Bark-peeling is at its best when birches are young – that is, between five and thirty years old – which is good news for anyone who wants to see concrete results in their lifetime.

Equally striking are the striped barks of the so-called snake-bark maples – *Acer capillipes*, *A. davidii*, and *A. pensylvanicum* – which hail originally from China or the eastern United States. Especially when young, the barks of these trees are spectacularly streaked silver and green.

Even barks that appear to be permanent do in fact change over time, often becoming more scored, marked, and fissured as the tree expands its girth and the living cells become further removed from the exterior. A surprisingly large number of woody plants have bark which, if not striking, is at least an interesting feature. A mature domestic apple tree, for example, is fissured in an intriguing way, an

attraction that is enhanced by the growth of silvery green lichen. An ash (*Fraxinus*) will have a smooth grey trunk when young, which becomes scored and lined after fifty years or so of growth. Both these trees are usually planted for reasons other than their bark, but learning to appreciate their colours and textures adds to our enjoyment of them.

The evergreen madrono (*Arbutus menziesii*), with its peeling red-brown bark, the superficially similar *Stewartia pseudocamellia*, and *Salix alba* subsp. *vitellina* 'Britzensis', with its bright orange-red winter shoots, must also be added to the list. As for the winged spindle (*Euonymus alatus*), although the bark is not highly coloured, its winged shape is eye-catching and highly ornamental, and makes it an excellent conversation piece.

Weather can affect the appearance of all barks. A heavy bout of rain will make a bark like that of *Prunus serrula* gleam like the polished wood of a Sheraton desk (hence its common name Sheraton cherry), while slanting winter sunlight can make a bark glow, as if lit from within.

This glow is also very evident in the brightly coloured young stems and branchlets of dogwoods: in *Cornus alba* 'Sibirica' and in *C. a.* 'Aurea' they are deep red or orange, while they are greenish yellow in *Cornus stolonifera* 'Flaviramea'. The young shoots of maples – *Acer griseum*, *A. palmatum* 'Sango-kaku', and the snake-bark maples, *A. capillipes* and *A. davidii* – have glistening red leaf shoots.

Bark on trees and shrubs can have striking colours or texture, and is an important identifying feature.
ABOVE LEFT *Arbutus* x *andrachnoides*.
ABOVE RIGHT *Betula papyrifera*.
LEFT *Betula albosinensis* var. *septentrionalis*, **here grown as a multi-stemmed plant.**

It is also possible to include a few border plants in this category of attractive coloured stems. For example, *Artemisia lactiflora* 'Guizhou' has purple-flushed stems, as well as young leaves; these stems make the plant look considerably darker and more sumptuous than the species *A. lactiflora*. *Eryngium bourgatii* would make far less impact in the border were it not for its shining blue stems.

Once you have become attuned to the possibilities of bark and stem colour and texture, there is even more you can do to increase its impact on the garden. Older birches, ornamental cherries, and maples, which are losing the freshness of clean bark, may be scrubbed with a dry scrubbing brush in winter to restrict the growth of lichen, and reveal the coloured bark beneath. It is unwise, however, to peel away a great deal of bark on birch trees prematurely, or you could damage the tree. It is much better, and more picturesque, to let it drop naturally.

The very youthful, glowing, smooth bark of several plants – dogwoods (*Cornus*) and willows (*Salix*), in particular – can be retained by techniques known as 'stooling' and 'pollarding'. Both genera will stand very hard pruning. With dogwoods, cut back the stems practically to ground level every other year in spring (this is known as stooling); with willows, cut back all the stems to about 1.5 m (5 ft) from the ground each spring, just before they come into leaf (pollarding). *Salix alba* subsp. *vitellina* 'Britzensis' and *Salix daphnoides* are particularly suitable candidates for pollarding.

As well as enhancing the colours of the bark, pollarding has the added attraction of being a reasonably safe way to restrict the growth of willows, which can be overpowering in medium or small gardens. Remember that pollarded and stooled trees can still have extensive, thirsty root systems.

Plants that respond positively to stooling include *Cornus alba*, *C. stolonifera* 'Flaviramea', *Eucalyptus gunnii*, and *Rubus cockburnianus*. The latter is an ornamental bramble grown mainly for its arching purple canes, overlaid with a white bloom, in winter. Its attractive ferny foliage, purple flowers in summer, and black fruit in autumn are all additional bonuses.

BELOW **The corky, winged stems of the winged spindle, *Euonymus alatus*, are clearly visible just as this marvellous shrub comes into leaf in spring.**

The various plants that have distinctive buds in winter are also of interest to the observant gardener. The willow shrub, *Salix fargesii*, has shining, sealing-wax red winter buds, and the enormous sticky buds of horse chestnut (*Aesculus hippocastanum*) are a wonder to children. Equally pleasurable are the thin, pointed, copper buds of beech (*Fagus sylvatica*), the triangular black buds of ash (*Fraxinus excelsior*), and the furry buds of apples (*Malus*).

It may seem far-fetched, but even thorns can be garden assets. For example, *Rosa sericea* subsp. *omeiensis* f. *pteracantha* combines very pretty, pale yellow single flowers in early summer, with distinctive and very striking thorns. These thorns are flat, triangular in shape, 3 cm (1¼in) wide by 2 cm (¾in) long, deep crimson in colour, and translucent; they will glow if planted where the sun will catch them. This attribute is especially obvious in winter, when many, or all, of the leaves have fallen. Regular pruning encourages the production of young shoots, which have the best coloured thorns. It must be said that once you begin considering the merits of a plant by the impact of its thorns, you are well on the way to becoming a discerning gardener!

OPPOSITE *Acer griseum*, the well-named paper-bark maple, amongst red and yellow stemmed cornus and a groundcover of *Hedera colchica* 'Sulphur Heart'.
ABOVE The curious striations on the trunk give this maple (*Acer pensylvanicum* 'Erythrocladum'), the name 'snake-bark'.
RIGHT The bright red winter stems of *Cornus alba* 'Sibirica' rise above *Helleborus foetidus* and *Erica* x *darleyensis* 'Furzey'.

HABIT

The shape of a plant and the way it grows – its 'habit' (or 'form') – are important features which we should not overlook when buying plants. The range of shapes is very wide, but a plant can also change shape, both during a season and in the course of its natural life.

Once the gardener becomes aware that there are other facets of plants besides flowers, a new world of possibilities opens up. Foliage, berries, and bark have important parts to play, but we should not forget that the shape of a plant and the way it grows can be positive features in themselves. This is what we call loosely a plant's 'habit'.

A plant's habit may have a strong influence on the atmosphere and appearance of a garden – or part of one – yet is often overlooked when choosing plants. It is rarely given much emphasis on plant labels, for example. Once we learn to appreciate this feature, however, we can start to be creative with plants, using their infinite variety of shapes to produce striking, often long-lasting combinations.

Trees are often described as broadly or narrowly conical, broadly or narrowly columnar, rounded, spreading, umbrella-like, weeping, or fastigiate (narrowly erect). Shrubs may be multi-stemmed, urn-shaped, prostrate, upright, arching, or even upright and arching. The range is considerable. Even border plants have their individual habits or 'personality', from prostrate to erect, from arching to vase-shaped, from dome-like to pendulous.

We can often tell a plant – even from a distance – just by its form. The arrangement and density of its branches or stems are often clues to its identity. Horse chestnut (*Aesculus*), birch (*Betula*), ash (*Fraxinus*), oak (*Quercus*),

ABOVE, LEFT TO RIGHT **Sedum 'Herbstfreude' (syn. 'Autumn Joy') is an herbaceous perennial, whose fleshy leaves are a fresh green in spring. In summer, the pale green flowers buds appear on the end of elongating stems, altering the plant's habit. In late summer, the plant changes again when in full flower.**

OPPOSITE **In a final change, by mid-autumn the sedum's flowers have set seed and the leaves are yellowing before they fall.**

and lime trees (*Tilia*), all reveal themselves in winter by the particular arrangement of the branches. We may not always be able to define the differences, but we can usually recognize them.

Another factor that affects the look of a plant is the arrangement of leaves on the stem. Some leaves – such as those of maples (*Acer*) – are borne in opposite pairs on either side of the stem. Others, like those of birches (*Betula*), are carried alternately. There are also other, more complex leaf arrangements. In apples (*Malus*), for example, the sixth leaf is vertically above the first on a shoot. The real reason for these leaf arrangements is to provide the best chance of exposure to the available sunlight, but they can have a great impact on the look of a plant as well.

The habit of a plant is usually influenced closely by how fast it grows. The red-barked dogwood (*Cornus alba*), for example, a fast grower, produces long, straight stems in the course of a season, whereas a slow grower like the common holly (*Ilex aquifolium*) has leaves and sideshoots very closely placed on the main stems.

For best effect, plants should be grown in groups that either reinforce their particular identity (a small grove of the flame-shaped *Carpinus betulus* 'Fastigiata', for example, or *Cornus sanguinea* 'Winter Beauty'), or contrast markedly with each other (*Skimmia japonica* with *Daphne mezereum*, or *Cotoneaster lacteus* and *Hydrangea quercifolia*).

Many trees and shrubs look as they do for the benefit of the gardener. A popular shape is clean-stemmed to 2 m (6 ft) tall, then with branches arising at more or less equal distances thereafter. This shape is usually aesthetically pleasing, and least likely to give practical problems, such as mowing around them, later on. Most people are familiar with the attractive shape of a mature cultivated apple tree, such as a 'Bramley'. A dual trunk, often divided about 1 m (3 ft) from the ground, produces a mass of out-spreading branches that create a kind of arboreal umbrella. It is a very satisfying shape, perhaps partly because it is traditional and therefore seems familiar to us.

Some plants seem to stamp their own personality on the garden without any help from the gardener. The Japanese maples (*Acer palmatum* and cultivars) and the cultivated sycamore (*Acer pseudoplatanus* 'Brilliantissimum') seem strictly genetically programmed to produce umbrella-shaped crowns. Among the evergreens, mahonias have a very particular erect and tiered look. *Viburnum plicatum* 'Mariesii' and, even more, *Cornus controversa* 'Horizontalis'

OPPOSITE **The wonderful 'wedding cake' habit
of *Cornus controversa* 'Variegata'.**
ABOVE **The prostrate habit of *Cotoneaster horizontalis*
contrasts with erect birch stems.**
RIGHT ***Stipa gigantea* erupting into flower in summer.**

also have an exceptional habit: no secateurs or pruning saw could ever ensure branches that stretch out so elegantly on a horizontal plane.

Although many plants will take on their own distinct form, you can do much to dictate their shape by judicious pruning. This is most marked with a hedge, where you plant a number of the same species in a straight line, and restrict their growth by annual pruning. Usually, in order to allow enough light and moisture to reach the bottom part, it is best to prune it in a pyramidal shape, i.e. narrower at the top than at the bottom. Although artificial, this form is both visually satisfying and practical. You can also turn a rounded shrub – *Chaenomeles* × *superba* 'Crimson and Gold', for example – into a wall plant by pruning off the shoots growing away from the wall, and tying in the others.

In the case of trees with attractive bark, there is a positive virtue in growing them as multi-stemmed shrubs, in preference to single-stemmed trees. This is achieved by cutting the main stem right back at an early age, so that several stems grow up to replace it. After all, it is the young, or youngish, wood of maples and birches that show the best colouring, so there is a lot to be said for multiplying the stems. A maple, having opposite rather than alternately arranged leaves, will often grow two branches from one place on the trunk in any event.

Close planting – in order to make an effective screen or windbreak, for example – can also alter the shape of a tree or large shrub. It is likely to produce fewer lower branches and more leaves at the top than a specimen tree, growing longer and thinner in order to compete successfully for light. You could use this natural occurrence to your advantage by planting several white-barked birches close together to maximize the impact of the bark, without the danger of too much shade being cast.

Habit and form move in and out of focus at different times of the year. They show up most clearly in winter, of course. The 'winter skeleton' is the name given to the shape of a tree or shrub (usually deciduous) without foliage, flowers, or berries. It is a constant for almost half the year, so it is vital that at least some plants offer interest in terms of structural form. Whatever the shape of a tree or shrub, ensure that its winter silhouette will be viewed to best advantage, either against a background of shining evergreens, or simply standing out against the open sky.

Plants with particularly fine winter skeletons include birches (*Betula*), because of the thin and flexible nature of the branches; any pendulous plant, such as the weeping birch (*Betula pendula* 'Youngii'), weeping beech (*Fagus sylvatica* 'Pendula'), weeping ash (*Fraxinus excelsior* 'Pendula'), and weeping pear (*Pyrus salicifolia* 'Pendula'); and any narrowly erect tree, such as *Carpinus betulus* 'Fastigiata' or *Fagus*

ABOVE AND LEFT *Halesia carolina* has branches that sweep attractively to the ground, in contrast to the upright habit of *Acer palmatum* 'Sango-kaku'.

sylvatica 'Dawyck'. These cultivars are particularly useful to the all-season gardener, because they take up less space in the garden than the species and so allow more variety.

A garden containing only deciduous plants can make for a bleak view on a dull day in winter, so it is vital to include some evergreens. In winter, we are much more conscious of the form and shape, say, of conifers, than at any other time of year, particularly if it snows or freezes. Their solidity is comforting when all the surrounding trees and shrubs are bare, and we are usually grateful for having included some in our plantings. The same is true of hollies (*Ilex*), the cherry laurel (*Prunus laurocerasus*), and the evergreen cotoneasters.

Other changes in habit may take place in the course of the season. The shape of a domestic apple tree may change when it is loaded down with a heavy crop of apples in early autumn, while a grass, such as *Helictotrichon sempervirens*, moves from being a low hummock to a vertical eruption when it flowers. On the whole, however, the shape of a plant is its most changeless attribute, often evident through all the seasons.

RIGHT **Betula pendula has a distinctive airy habit.**
BELOW **A group of grasses together shows how varying habits complement each other.**

plants for all seasons

SHRUBS

Shrubs, like trees, often provide structure and an appearance of permanence to a garden, but they can also offer a degree of changeability. Deciduous shrubs can, of course, alter out of all recognition in the course of the growing season, but evergreens, some of which are included here, can also exhibit enormous variety.

BELOW **The fragrant, frost-resistant flowers of *Hamamelis* x *intermedia* 'Jelena' will always brighten the winter garden.**

JAPANESE BARBERRY
Berberis thunbergii 'Rose Glow'

There are many good cultivars of *Berberis thunbergii*, but none is more popular than 'Rose Glow'. The attractiveness of this small deciduous shrub lies mainly in the leaves and, perhaps to a lesser degree, in the flowers. When the leaves first appear, they resemble closely those of *B. thunbergii* 'Atropurpurea', being small, obovate, and dark reddish purple. Gradually, however, young leaves appear with white, silver and pink markings; they lose their variegation as they age and, in autumn, turn a rich scarlet-red before they fall. The small, drooping flowers, borne in spring, are pale yellow, suffused with orange, and are followed by small ovoid berries, which become bright red. 'Rose Glow' is always a compact, dense, spiny shrub, which can be used to make a slow-growing, short hedge or, if clipped, a specimen. Other similar *Berberis thunbergii* cultivars include 'Harlequin'; 'Pink Queen', with more heavily variegated leaves; and 'Silver Beauty', with creamy white markings.

ABOVE LEFT **The young leaves of** *Berberis* **'Rose Glow' are spattered with silver, pink and white markings. These fade to purple with age.**

ABOVE RIGHT **A further transition occurs in autumn, when the leaves offer reliably spectacular red tints.**

Habit: rounded, dense, stiff
Height: 1.5m (5ft)
Spread: up to 1.5m (5ft)
Flowering season: spring
Origin of species: Japan
Hardiness: fully hardy UK; Zone 4 US
Cultivation: plant in a sunny position in any well-drained soil. Prune in late autumn or late winter. Take softwood cuttings in early summer, or semi-ripe, heeled cuttings in late summer.

BEAUTY BERRY
Callicarpa bodinieri var. *giraldii* 'Profusion'

The beauty berry is a medium-sized to large deciduous shrub grown for its distinctive clusters of very long-lasting, lustrous violet-purple berries and purple-tinged foliage in autumn, and its bronze-coloured leaves in spring. Of all the beauty berries, *Callicarpa bodinieri* var. *giraldii* 'Profusion' is the most commonly grown; it is aptly named, producing more fruit than the species. 'Profusion' makes a bushy shrub, with large, downy, dark green, obovate, tapered leaves, and

tiny, star-shaped pink flowers in small cymes in the leaf axils in midsummer. The berries are small, up to 4mm (⅛in) across, spherical, and like clusters of little beads. This is a choice shrub for a prominent position, where it can get plenty of sunshine to promote good berry production in autumn. The best crops of berries are produced where these plants are grown in groups (because they cross-pollinate), and after a long, hot summer.

ABOVE LEFT **The violet-purple berries and purple-tinged leaves create a striking and unusual combination in autumn.**
ABOVE RIGHT **The flowers are tiny individually, but form attractive, brightly coloured clusters in midsummer.**

Habit: rounded, upright
Height: up to 3m (10ft)
Spread: 2–2.5m (6–8ft)
Flowering season: midsummer
Origin of species: China
Hardiness: fully hardy UK; Zone 6 US
Cultivation: a sunny, sheltered place is best in a fertile, well-drained soil. Cut the shrub back in early spring. Take softwood cuttings in spring, or semi-ripe, heeled cuttings in summer.

COMMON HEATHER, LING
Calluna vulgaris 'Robert Chapman'

There are literally hundreds of cultivars of *Calluna vulgaris*, which are worthy of a place in any garden where the soil is neutral or acid. They make excellent evergreen groundcover for many years, provided they are trimmed over from time to time to prevent them from becoming too tall and straggly. 'Robert Chapman', a widely available cultivar, offers both late summer and autumn flowers and excellent winter foliage. The flowers are single and a soft purple. The summer foliage is golden but turns orange and then red as the days shorten; throughout winter, it makes a bright display. This heather can be grown successfully as a rock garden specimen or as groundcover.

Habit: upright, groundcovering
Height: 30cm (12in)
Spread: up to 65cm (26in)
Flowering season: late summer to autumn
Origin of species: Europe, including Britain
Hardiness: fully hardy UK; Zone 5 US
Cultivation: likes a poor, free-draining, but not droughty, neutral or acid soil, with added peat, in full sun. These shrubs are best trimmed over in spring, especially if the soil is fertile. Propagation is by layering in spring or by division or semi-ripe heeled cuttings in summer.

ABOVE RIGHT **The foliage forms a sea of gold in summer. Towards the end of the season, the impact is even greater as the contrasting purple flowers emerge.**
RIGHT **The colours of the foliage deepen throughout autumn. By winter, the orange and red leaves make a dazzling display.**

INDIAN BEAN TREE
Catalpa bignonioides 'Aurea'

The well-known Indian bean tree, *Catalpa bignonioides*, is a fine deciduous specimen tree with a distinctive umbrella shape. One of its main attributes is the large, heart-shaped foliage, which is characteristically late to open in spring. The leaves can be as much as 30cm (12in) long and 20cm (8in) wide, and give off a smell when crushed. The foxglove-shaped flowers are upright and white, with yellow and mauve markings, and appear in high summer. After hot summers, they are followed by bunches of slender green bean pods, up to 35cm (14in) long, which blacken as they mature and persist over winter. It is possible to stool these trees so that they can be grown in a shrub border; as a result, the leaves will be even bigger than usual. *C. bignonioides* 'Aurea' is the cultivar with leaves which begin bronze, then turn bright yellow and, finally, lime-green in summer.

Habit: domed, spreading
Height: up to 12m (40ft)
Spread: up to 10m (30ft)
Flowering season: mid- to late summer
Origin of species: North America
Hardiness: fully hardy UK; Zone 5 US
Cultivation: this tree should be planted in a sheltered place, so that the wind cannot damage its enormous leaves. It will grow best in a moist but well-drained, fertile soil in full sun. Young plants need protection from winter cold. If the plant is to be stooled to make a shrub, cut the stems back hard in early spring to within three buds of the base. Propagation is by softwood cuttings in summer, or by grafting in winter.

ABOVE LEFT The large, handsome leaves make a great impact on the garden from spring to autumn, while the umbrella-shaped habit forms a focal point throughout the year.
LEFT The foxglove-like flowers are carried in panicles in high summer.

DOGWOOD
Cornus 'Eddie's White Wonder'

This beautiful dogwood, a hybrid between *C. florida* and *C. nuttallii*, makes a large deciduous shrub or small tree, with a conical, upright habit. Its flowers, produced in late spring, are typical of other dogwoods: four to six rounded, pure-white bracts surrounding a knob of purplish green flowers. The ovate leaves have wavy edges, and are glossy green, taking on red and orange tints before they fall. Other excellent flowering dogwoods include *Cornus florida* 'Cherokee Chief', with dark red bracts; *C. kousa* var. *chinensis*, with flaking bark and white bracts that turn red-pink; and the very vigorous *C. nuttallii* 'Colrigo Giant'. All dogwoods are potentially excellent garden plants. They are not suitable for all situations, but provided they are planted in the right place, and the soil is enriched, they are worthwhile.

ABOVE LEFT **It is the showy white bracts, sometimes up to 8cm (3in) long, that steal the show rather than the insignificant purplish green flowers at the centre.**
ABOVE RIGHT **The leaves turn to fiery shades of orange and red in autumn.**

Habit: upright, broadly conical
Height: up to 6m (20ft)
Spread: up to 5m (15ft)
Flowering season: late spring
Origin: garden origin
Hardiness: fully hardy UK; Zone 6 US
Cultivation: flowering dogwoods like sun or light shade, sheltered from strong winds and spring frosts, and a fertile, well-drained, neutral or acid soil. Pruning is usually unnecessary. They may be propagated by semi-ripe cuttings in summer, but are usually grafted in winter.

CORNELIAN CHERRY
Cornus mas

Good hardy, winter-flowering shrubs are few and far between, so the Cornelian cherry is a must, provided there is sufficient space for it to grow and spread. It has showy but small clusters of yellow-green flowers in late winter, before the leaves appear; a good specimen will be almost literally covered in them. The flowers are succeeded by edible red fruit, not unlike elongated cherries (hence the common name), although these may be produced rather sparsely. The small, ovate, dark green dogwood leaves turn to red or purple in the autumn. There are both variegated ('Variegata') and yellow-leaved ('Aurea') cultivars, which are less vigorous than the species, but are highly ornamental. All look stunning against a background of evergreen trees or shrubs. This is a very amenable plant, thriving in a lime soil, in sun or partial shade. It is slow growing, and begins as an upright shrub, gradually spreading with age.

Habit: erect at first, then spreading and open
Height: up to 5m (15ft)
Spread: up to 5m (15ft)
Flowering season: late winter to early spring
Origin: central and southern Europe
Hardiness: fully hardy UK; Zone 5 US
Cultivation: this plant will thrive even in a very alkaline soil, and in sun or partial shade. It can be pruned in late winter either to produce a spreading, multi-stemmed shrub, or a fan-shaped tree. Propagation is by seed in autumn, or grafting in winter.

ABOVE LEFT *Cornus mas* in autumn.
LEFT **The flower heads open in late winter.**
BELOW **The shrub is smothered in a glorious mass of yellow-green flowers.**

COMMON DOGWOOD
Cornus sanguinea 'Winter Beauty'

Space should be found in every garden for a common dogwood. They are suckering shrubs that create enormous interest in winter: when the leaves have fallen, the spotlight falls on the very striking young stems which, in 'Winter Beauty', are glowing orange and red. Even in summer, when the stems are effectively hidden, these plants continue to draw the eye, producing flat clusters of small white flowers, usually followed by blue-black, spherical berries. Common dogwoods look best if grown in groups, associating well with other barked dogwoods, like the greenish yellow *C. stolonifera* 'Flaviramea' and the red-stemmed *C. alba* 'Sibirica'. Variegated and yellow-leaved cultivars, such as *C. alba* 'Elegantissima' and *C. a.* 'Aurea', also look good with them. Common dogwoods are excellent shrubs for the bog garden or the waterside.

ABOVE LEFT **The distinctively wavy dogwood leaves turn a pleasant golden-yellow in autumn before they fall.**
ABOVE RIGHT **The orange and red young stems glow in winter sunshine, and can be cut for indoor decoration.**

Habit: upright, suckering
Height: 3m (10ft), if unpruned
Spread: 2.5m (8ft)
Flowering season: early summer
Origin of species: Europe
Hardiness: fully hardy UK; Zone 4 US
Cultivation: these dogwoods are happy in most soils, including very moist ones, so are often planted near water. To ensure good stem colour, grow them in full sun, and prune plants hard every other year, in late winter or early spring. They are easily propagated by hardwood cuttings or division of suckers in winter.

Cotoneaster lacteus

This is a magnificent evergreen shrub for the larger garden. It has an impressively tall and arching habit, and produces milky white flowers, much loved by bees, in early summer. More importantly, the flowers are followed by masses of long-lasting, orange-red, ovoid berries in autumn and winter. The leathery leaves are unique among cotoneasters in being felted on the underside. They are dark green on the upper surface, obovate and conspicuously veined. *Cotoneaster lacteus* looks good as a specimen shrub and associates well with other shrubs; it can also be grown as a tall hedge. It grows happily in an exposed position, except in very cold conditions. Other recommended evergreen cotoneasters include *C. frigidus* 'Cornubia', which has larger fruit, and *C. sternianus*, with blue-green leaves and orange-red berries.

Habit: dense, arching, with pendulous stems
Height: 4m (12ft)
Spread: 3m (10ft)
Flowering season: early summer
Origin: China
Hardiness: fully hardy UK; Zone 7 US
Cultivation: it is very easy to grow, being suited to a variety of soils and sites (it will thrive in sun or partial shade), and tolerant of air pollution. In very cold areas, plant in a sheltered place. Pruning is rarely necessary for specimen shrubs, but they can be trimmed after flowering to tidy the shape up. Hedges should be cut after fruiting. Propagation is by semi-ripe cuttings in late summer, or seed in autumn. Like all cotoneasters, it is susceptible to a potentially fatal disease, called fireblight.

ABOVE LEFT **Abundant clusters of white flowers are borne on arching shoots in summer. They set fruit easily.**
LEFT **A close-up of the orange-red berries in late autumn, profusely held in bunches just above the evergreen foliage.**

Daphne mezereum

This small deciduous shrub flowers on naked, upright stems in late winter. The flowers are four-lobed, tubular, purplish pink and – like so many winter-flowerers – immensely fragrant. They are borne either singly or in small groups, and are followed in summer by glossy, red, round berries. The leaves, which appear after the flowers, are small, pale green, and oval or lance-shaped. There is a white form (f. *alba*), which has creamy yellow berries, and also a dark pink variety called *Daphne mezereum* var. *rubra*. All parts of *D. mezereum* are poisonous. It is prone to dying off in a few years, but usually seedlings will have sprung up nearby to replace it. There are many other very showy daphnes, also with fragrant flowers, such as *D. bholua* (flowering later in winter), *D.* x *burkwoodii* 'Somerset' (late spring), and *D. tangutica* (late spring and early summer).

ABOVE LEFT **This daphne is a superb winter performer, with intensely fragrant flowers and a strong, upright habit.**
ABOVE RIGHT **Berries are not usually very freely borne, but in summer this is a handsome foliage shrub in any event.**
LEFT **The glossy red berries are held in bunches close to the stems.**

Habit: upright
Height: up to 1.2m (4ft)
Spread: 80–100cm (32–39in)
Flowering season: late winter
Origin: Europe, including Britain, Turkey
Hardiness: fully hardy UK; Zone 5 US
Cultivation: grow in a humus-rich, acid or alkaline soil, preferably in partial shade. It does not transplant well, so buy a containerized plant. Pruning is rarely necessary. Sow seed when ripe, or take semi-ripe cuttings in summer. Virus can weaken the plant and yellow the leaves.

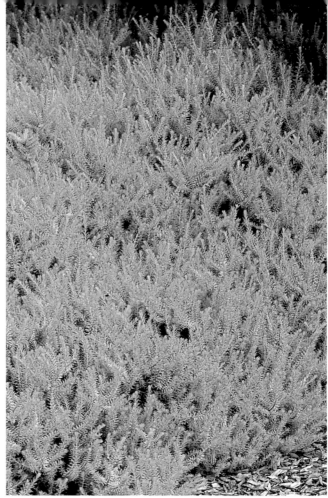

WINTER HEATH
Erica carnea 'Golden Starlet'

There are dozens of excellent cultivars of the winter-flowering heath, *Erica carnea*. Their great virtue is that they will tolerate an alkaline soil, so offer an opportunity for all gardeners to grow excellent evergreen ground cover. 'Golden Starlet' is a choice variety because it has good white flowers in late winter and early spring, together with complementary lime-green foliage; as the season wears on to summer, this takes on a bright yellow hue. If planted *en masse*, it creates a striking effect, either in the rock garden or as groundcover around deciduous shrubs. 'Golden Starlet' is particularly unusual because it does not mix yellow foliage with pink or purple flowers, as is the more common combination. Other *E. carnea* cultivars include 'King George', with pink flowers in early winter; 'Myretoun Ruby', with pink flowers that turn red with age; and the vigorous, trailing, white-flowered 'Springwood White'. However, these do not have the added bonus of foliage that changes colour.

ABOVE LEFT **The small, neat, urn-shaped flowers are only 6mm (¼in) long, but are carried in profusion.**
ABOVE RIGHT **The lime-green foliage of winter gradually turns golden yellow by summertime.**

Habit: groundcovering
Height: about 20cm (8in)
Spread: about 50cm (20in)
Flowering season: late winter to early spring
Origin of species: European Alps
Hardiness: fully hardy UK; Zone 5 US
Cultivation: heaths are best planted in a sunny, open position away from trees. They like a well-drained soil, and will tolerate lime. Plant deeply, even covering the lowest leaves, to keep them neat in later years. Trim them over immediately after flowering. To propagate, take semi-ripe, heeled cuttings in summer.

WINGED SPINDLE
Euonymus alatus

The winged spindle is a must for anyone who gardens on an alkaline soil, for it combines glorious and reliable autumn leaf colour with colourful berries and a distinctive branching habit. The leaves are deciduous, dark green, ovate and toothed, and become a deep pinkish red colour in autumn. There are flowers, too, but these are insignificant. The berries, on the other hand, can be showy: spherical, reddish purple, and four-lobed, they usually split open to reveal four orange seeds, although often some of these do not develop. The common name refers to the four corky 'wings' present on each shoot. That attribute adds to the charm and distinction of the bare shrub in the winter. Another good euonymus, renowned for its autumn colour, is *E. europaeus* 'Red Cascade'. There are also a number of evergreen euonymus, often with variegated foliage, such as cultivars of *E. fortunei*.

Habit: dense, many-branched, spreading
Height: up to 2.5m (8ft)
Spread: up to 3m (10ft)
Flowering season: late spring to early summer
Origin: China, Japan
Hardiness: fully hardy UK; Zone 4 US
Cultivation: it will grow in any ordinary soil, including chalk, in sun or semi-shade. It berries most profusely when grown together with others in a group, so that cross-fertilization can take place. Pruning is rarely necessary, except to remove crossing or congested branches in late winter. Propagate by sowing seed in autumn when it is ripe (this can be a very slow process), or by taking softwood cuttings in summer.

ABOVE RIGHT **The spring flowers are hard to see because they are so small, but both the spring foliage and the habit are attractive.** RIGHT **Stunning autumn leaf colour is accompanied by berries, which open to reveal showy orange seeds.**

JAPANESE ARALIA
Fatsia japonica

A balanced and successful garden planting requires that some plants are a constant presence, always impressive but taking centre stage only for a limited spell. An excellent candidate for this position is *Fatsia japonica*, an evergreen shrub with very striking foliage, which flowers in autumn. It looks like a gigantic shrubby ivy, with its dark green, shiny leaves, up to 30cm (12in) across, cut into seven or nine very distinct lobes, and small, five-petalled, flowers in branching umbels. These are followed by black spherical fruits. This is a most impressive plant, particularly when it reaches 3 or 4m (10 or 12ft) high, but it is not very hardy and needs a warm sheltered place outside, such as in a walled garden or courtyard. Its great virtues are that it will grow in either sun or partial shade, and its glossy leaves are immune to pests or damage by pollution or salt-laden spray. There is a variegated cultivar, 'Variegata', which is slower growing and needs an even warmer spot in the garden.

ABOVE LEFT **The fascinating finger-like leaves of *Fatsia japonica* are a stunning, year-round feature of this shrub.**
ABOVE RIGHT **The tiny autumn flowers in rounded heads reveal the relationship between this shrub and the ivy family.**

Habit: rounded, spreading
Height: up to 4m (12ft)
Spread: up to 3m (10ft)
Flowering season: autumn
Origin: Japan, South Korea
Hardiness: frost hardy UK; Zone 8 US
Cultivation: this plant likes a sheltered position in sun or partial shade, and a well-drained, reasonably fertile soil. Its general tolerance and slight tenderness make it an ideal city plant. Pruning is generally unnecessary. Take softwood cuttings in early summer.

MOUNTAIN WITCH HAZEL
Fothergilla major

The mountain witch hazel is a deciduous shrub that combines stunning autumn leaf colour with unusual and attractive flowers. It makes an upright shrub, usually no more than 2.5m (8ft) tall, many-branched, dense and rounded in shape. It is quite slow growing. In late spring, vertical spikes of scented white, or pink-tinged, 'flowers' appear before, and with the leaves, and occasionally again in autumn. These flowers are, in fact, without petals, consisting instead simply of stamens. The leaves are obovate and toothed, and turn to tints of yellow, orange and red in autumn. This is a plant for a woodland situation, or border, in a neutral or acid soil.

Habit: rounded, densely branched
Height: up to 2.5m (8ft)
Spread: up to 2m (6ft)
Flowering season: late spring
Origin: south-eastern USA
Hardiness: fully hardy UK; Zone 5 US
Cultivation: this plant thrives in a moist, acid soil, with plenty of leafmould. It colours best in full sun, provided the soil does not dry out in summer. Pruning is rarely necessary. To propagate, sow seed when it is ripe in autumn; it may take 18 months to germinate. Alternatively, layer in autumn or take softwood cuttings in summer.

ABOVE RIGHT **The fragrant, bottlebrush-like flowers are the main feature of this shrub in late spring and early summer.**
RIGHT **In autumn, the brilliant leaf colour takes over. The colours are best if the plant is in a sunny site with moisture-retentive soil.**

CHECKERBERRY, WINTERGREEN
Gaultheria procumbens

The checkerberry, or wintergreen, is a creeping, ground-cover plant for an acid soil and partial shade. Although not a truly striking shrub, it has a quiet charm. Its main attractions are the pendulous, urn-shaped small flowers, either white or pale pink and usually borne in clusters in summer, and the round, scarlet, aromatic fruit that follows. It also has neat, carpeting, glossy evergreen foliage, which smells of wintergreen when bruised or crushed; this plant was once used for the extraction of 'oil of wintergreen'. The leaves are small, oval or elliptic, and toothed, with a leathery texture, and take on purple tones in cold weather. This plant colonizes ground by the use of its underground stems, called rhizomes, but is not really invasive. It is suitable for planting in woodland or in a rock garden, or on a peat bank, and is useful in shady sites.

Habit: creeping
Height: 15cm (6in)
Spread: about 1m (3ft)
Flowering season: mid- to late summer
Origin: eastern North America
Hardiness: fully hardy UK; Zone 3 US
Cultivation: it needs an acid or neutral, moist soil, preferably in partial shade. Trim lightly after flowering if necessary. Propagation is by seed sown when ripe, or division in autumn. These divisions are best put in pots initially for good roots to form. Semi-ripe cuttings can also be taken in summer.

ABOVE LEFT **In autumn and winter, the leaves take on a purple tinge, and bright red berries appear: the extent of colour change and fruit production depends on the temperature.**
LEFT **The flowers are small and urn-shaped, and appear in summer. They are not always very freely borne.**

SNOWDROP TREE
Halesia carolina

The snowdrop trees are a charming genus of large deciduous shrubs or small trees, so-named because they produce masses of pendulous, pure-white, snowdrop-like flowers in late spring or early summer. One of the most suitable for the garden is *Halesia carolina*, whose nodding, bell-shaped flowers, 2cm (¾in) long, hang in clusters of three or five on short stalks, just before the leaves appear in spring. A well-covered plant is a spectacular sight. The autumn fruits are highly intriguing: they are pear-shaped with four wings, and 5cm (2in) long.

They begin green but gradually turn to brown as they ripen. The large leaves are ovate with pointed ends, and mid-green, turning yellow in autumn. *H. carolina* is an excellent subject for a large shrub border, or as a specimen. It is reasonably slow growing, and will take a few years before it flowers freely. Other good varieties are *H. diptera* var. *magniflora*, with large flowers, and *H. monticola* var. *vestita*, which makes more of a tree. The disadvantage of halesias is that they will not grow happily in alkaline soils.

ABOVE LEFT **The exquisite beauty of the 'snowdrop' flowers of *Halesia carolina* is undeniable. They are carried in profusion in clusters of three or five.**

ABOVE RIGHT **It is hard to believe that the lovely petals fall to reveal such quirky four-winged fruits in autumn.**

Habit: spreading
Height: 3m (10ft)
Spread: about 3m (10ft)
Flowering season: late spring
Origin: south-eastern USA
Hardiness: fully hardy UK; Zone 4 US
Cultivation: plant in a fertile, moist but well-drained, neutral or acid soil, in sun or semi-shade, in a spot away from cold winds. Pruning is rarely necessary. Propagation is by layering young branches in spring, or by rooting softwood cuttings in summer.

OAK-LEAVED HYDRANGEA
Hydrangea quercifolia

The oak-leaved hydrangea is worthy of a place in the garden for the unusual shape of its leaves, its very reliable autumn colour, and its late summer flowers. It is a choice, medium-sized, deciduous shrub, which grows to a maximum of 2.5m (8ft), but spreads by ground-creeping stems to 3.5m (11ft) or more. The foliage is particularly striking, being very big and lobed, and resembles the leaves of some oak species, hence the common name; it is dark green and leathery in texture. In autumn, before the leaves fall, they turn various shades of scarlet, purple and orange. The creamy flower heads (a mixture of sterile and fertile flowers) are conical in shape, sometimes up to 30cm (12in) long but often smaller, and turn pink as they age. There are two other recommended and readily available cultivars, 'Snow Flake', which has attractive double flowers, and the profusely flowering 'Snow Queen'. *Hydrangea paniculata* is another excellent late-summer hydrangea with conical creamy white flower heads.

OPPOSITE The large, striking leaves of this hydrangea are unique, but strongly resemble those of an oak.

ABOVE LEFT As the season wears on, the flowers gradually change from creamy white to pink or pale purple.

ABOVE RIGHT The depth and range of the autumn colour depend to a large extent on soil and climate, but can be magnificent.

Habit: mound-shaped, spreading
Height: 2.5m (8ft)
Spread: 3.5m (11ft) or more
Flowering season: late summer
Origin: south-eastern USA
Hardiness: fully hardy UK; Zone 5 US
Cultivation: grow in a humus-rich, moisture-retentive soil in light shade, preferably sheltered from cold winds. Remove only dead wood in winter and crossing branches in spring. Propagate by softwood cuttings in early summer, or hardwood cuttings in winter.

WITCH HAZEL
Hamamelis × *intermedia* 'Jelena'

Hamamelis, or witch hazel, is a wonderful genus of deciduous small trees or large, multi-stemmed shrubs, with excellent autumn leaf colour and spidery, fragrant, frost-resistant flowers in winter. *Hamamelis* × *intermedia* 'Jelena' is a particularly fine cultivar, derived from a cross between *H. mollis* and *H. japonica*. The flowers, 3cm (1¼in) across, are composed of four ribbon-like, wavy petals, held in dense clusters close to the bare stems. They are yellow, tinged with coppery red, and make a brave show even on very cold days. The leaves, which unfurl in spring, are hazel-like: obovate, deeply ridged, hairy, and capable of turning lovely shades of scarlet and orange in autumn. The cultivars of *H.* × *intermedia* tend to have upward-growing branches, so make vase-shaped shrubs. They are best grown as specimens, against a dark background to show up the flowers in winter.

Habit: vase-shaped, spreading
Height: up to 4m (12ft)
Spread: up to 3m (10ft)
Flowering season: mid- to late winter
Origin: garden origin
Hardiness: fully hardy UK; Zone 5 US
Cultivation: it is best grown in a humus-rich, neutral to acid soil, in sun or partial shade, but will grow in a lime soil, provided it is deep and rich. Remove only dead wood. It is propagated by grafting in winter.

ABOVE LEFT **This witch hazel is the queen of winter-flowering shrubby trees. Although it is regrettably slow growing, it is well worth the wait.**
LEFT **Witch hazels are renowned also for their brilliant autumn colour.**

ST JOHN'S WORT
Hypericum × *inodorum* 'Elstead'

The interesting feature of *Hypericum* × *inodorum* 'Elstead' is that the flowers and fruit may be seen on the plant at the same time. This produces a most unusual colour combination of yellow and pink; while this is not to everyone's taste, it is certainly distinctive.

Hypericum × *inodorum* 'Elstead', derived from a cross between *H. androsaemum* and *H. hircinum*, makes a 1.2m (4ft) high, deciduous or semi-evergreen shrub, with dark green, ovate or lance-shaped leaves.

In summer, the bush is well covered in clusters of yellow, saucer-like flowers with distinctive bristles of protruding stamens, up to 3cm (1¼in) across. As the summer wears on, these flowers slowly develop into ovoid fruits, first whitish pink in colour, then darkening to a bright orange-red. This is not a truly choice plant but, because of its long-lasting flowers and fruit, and its willingness to grow in shade, it is an extremely useful one.

ABOVE LEFT **These are typical St John's wort flowers with prominent, protruding stamens. Other species and cultivars, such as** *Hypericum calycinum* **and 'Rowallane', have larger flowers.**
ABOVE RIGHT **The long-lasting berries undergo a change in colour from whitish pink to bright orange-red.**

Habit: erect
Height: up to 1.2m (4ft)
Spread: up to 1.2m (4ft)
Flowering season: midsummer to mid-autumn
Origin: garden origin
Hardiness: fully hardy UK; Zone 7 US
Cultivation: this hypericum will grow in any reasonably fertile soil in sun or shade. Trim stems back in spring. Propagate by semi-ripe cuttings in summer. The only problem is a disfiguring fungal disease called 'rust', which necessitates the removal of affected leaves.

ENGLISH HOLLY
Ilex aquifolium 'Argentea Marginata'

This is an extremely popular variegated-leaved holly, and rightly so. Not only has it been in gardens for a long time, but it is a striking and reliable evergreen shrub or tree that changes through the seasons. The species, *Ilex aquifolium*, has thick, ovate leaves with spiny, wavy edges. It bears male and female flowers on different plants. But 'Argentea Marginata' differs from the species in that the leaves are not as spiky or wavy, and they have a very pretty, broad, cream edging to them. The leaves are ovate, and generally about 7cm (2½in) long; the new leaves have a distinctive purple or pink tinge to them, which is very attractive. This cultivar is female, so fruiting is assured provided there are males nearby; indeed, the bright red berries are profuse. 'Argentea Marginata Pendula' has a weeping habit, which makes it a more suitable choice for a small garden. Other excellent variegated hollies (all *Ilex aquifolium* cultivars) include 'Handsworth New Silver', a dense shrub with dark purple stems, and 'Silver Milkmaid' with an open habit and silvery white leaf markings. A good plain evergreen is 'J.C. van Tol', because its leaves have very few prickles and it is self-fertile, so berries even when grown in isolation. Hollies are generally slow growing, especially in heavy soils. They make a very dense and effective hedge or topiary specimen.

ABOVE LEFT **The young leaves are tinged with pink or purple. This gradually fades as the leaves mature.**
ABOVE RIGHT **This female variety of holly berries very freely.**

Habit: columnar
Height: up to 15m (50ft), but usually smaller
Spread: 3m (10ft)
Flowering season: spring to early summer
Origin of species: western and southern Europe, north Africa, west Asia
Hardiness: fully hardy UK; Zone 6 US
Cultivation: grow this holly in a moist, fertile soil. Those planted in full sun get the brightest variegation. If grown as a specimen, this holly needs little pruning. If grown as a hedge, trim in early spring. Propagate by taking semi-ripe cuttings in late summer.

JAPANESE KERRIA
Kerria japonica 'Picta'

No one could consider *Kerria japonica* a choice shrub, for it is too easily and commonly grown. It is, however, extremely useful because of its early, bright butter-yellow flowers, its green stems in winter, and autumn colour.

Kerria japonica 'Picta' (syn. 'Variegata') combines these virtues, and adds to them pretty variegated leaves. The result is a smaller, but charming, amenable, suckering shrub. The deciduous leaves are grey-green with creamy white edges, and are ovate, pointed, and conspicuously toothed. In autumn, they are tinged yellow. The flowers are single, saucer-shaped, about 3cm (1¼in) across, and borne over many weeks in spring, with sometimes a second flush in autumn. All kerrias can be trained against a wall.

Habit: upright, arching, many-stemmed
Height: 1.5m (5ft)
Spread: 2m (6ft)
Flowering season: spring
Origin of species: China, Japan
Hardiness: fully hardy UK; Zone 5 US
Cultivation: grow in well-drained, fertile soil, in sun or partial shade. Prune after flowering, cutting back flowered shoots to strong new buds. Dig up outer stems and replant in autumn, or take cuttings in summer

TOP **The individual flowers of this kerria are charming; the petals are notched.**
TOP RIGHT **The variegated cultivar 'Picta' is not seen as often as the double cultivar 'Pleniflora', but it is more elegant.**
RIGHT **The leaves take on yellow tints before they fall.**

Mahonia japonica

This is a very fine evergreen winter-flowering shrub, with a tall, upright habit and a stately appearance. Its holly-like leaves are a great asset: intensely glossy, deep green and leathery in texture, and composed of numerous spiny, roughly ovate leaflets. The older leaves turn brilliant scarlet in autumn and winter, and can take on marbling at other times of the year as well. In early winter, intensely scented, lemon-yellow flowers, up to 25cm (10in) long, appear in spreading or drooping clusters at the ends of the shoots. The flowers open from the base up over a period of weeks, and are excellent for cutting. They continue until early spring, and are followed by ovoid, bloomy, bluish purple fruit, like small grapes. This plant can be grown as a specimen, as a handsome denizen of a shrub border, or together with others to make an informal windbreak. Unlike some mahonias, *M. japonica* is very hardy. Other good mahonias include *M. x media* 'Charity', with densely clustered, late autumn to late winter yellow flowers; 'Winter Sun' with bright yellow flowers; and 'Underway', which is more compact.

Habit: erect
Height: up to 2m (6ft)
Spread: up to 3m (10ft)
Flowering season: early winter to spring
Origin: China
Hardiness: fully hardy UK; Zone 7 US
Cultivation: grow in any reasonably fertile soil in partial shade. No pruning is necessary. Propagate by chilling seed outside in the winter and sowing in spring, or by taking semi-ripe cuttings in summer.

OPPOSITE ABOVE **In late autumn, some of the leaves of this evergreen shrub take on scarlet tints.**
OPPOSITE BELOW **The lemon-yellow flowers open from the base over many weeks; they are intensely fragrant.**
ABOVE RIGHT **Bloomy bluish purple fruits are evident in early summer.**
RIGHT **Even when not in flower, this evergreen shrub is very handsome.**

Photinia x *fraseri* 'Red Robin'

This underrated shrub, derived from a cross between *P. glabra* and *P. serratifolia*, should be more widely planted, for it provides superb leaf colour in spring and summer, and yet is evergreen; it makes a substantial upright but spreading plant, yet can be used for hedging; and it is happy in either acid or alkaline soils. Although it has attractive clusters, up to 15cm (6in) across, of white flowers in mid- and late spring, sometimes up to 15cm (6in) across, the true glory of this shrub is the glossy, leathery foliage, lance-shaped or oval and sharply toothed, which is shining bright red in spring, and again in late summer, later turning green. The young leaves are prone to damage in frost pockets, so this shrub should be planted against a wall or in the shelter of other shrubs; in warm districts, however, it makes excellent dense hedging. The leaves of 'Robusta' are more copper-red. Other cultivars you may come across include the bushy-headed *P.* x *fraseri* 'Birmingham', which sometimes has red fruit; and *P.* 'Redstart', which has red-orange berries.

ABOVE LEFT **In spring, the young leaves emerge brilliant red and only very gradually fade to dark green.**
ABOVE RIGHT **The shrub produces a flush of red young leaves in late summer.**

Habit: upright
Height: up to 3m (10ft)
Spread: 2–3m (6–10ft)
Flowering season: mid- to late spring
Origin: garden origin
Hardiness: basically hardy UK, but young growth prone to damage from frost; Zone 7 US
Cultivation: plant in sun or partial shade in a fertile, moist soil in a place sheltered from cold winds and hard frosts. The leaf colour can be improved by pruning in the dormant season. Propagate by ripewood cuttings in autumn.

Rhododendron luteum

One of the drawbacks of rhododendrons is that they are generally not scented, but that is definitely not the case with *Rhododendron luteum*, which can fill a woodland ride with its sweet perfume. Although grown mainly for its lovely yellow flowers, this deciduous azalea can also boast excellent autumn leaf colour. The sticky, funnel-shaped blooms, about 3.5cm (1½in) long, are borne in trusses containing up to 12 flowers. They appear in late spring and early summer. The leaves are oblong or lance-shaped, mid-green and hairy; they turn purple, crimson and orange before they fall. *Rhododendron luteum* makes a large shrub, about 3m (10ft) tall, and as much across. It is ideal for a woodland garden in acid soil, grown in a group, but it is also excellent in a very large container in ericaceous compost, placed in a sheltered spot in partial shade or full sun. Other attractive fragrant azaleas are *R. occidentale* and *R. viscosum*.

Habit: open
Height: 3m (10ft)
Spread: up to 3m (10ft)
Flowering season: late spring to early summer
Origin: Caucasus, eastern Europe
Hardiness: fully hardy UK; Zone 6 US
Cultivation: plant shallowly in a moist but well-drained, humus-rich, acid soil, in shelter and in light shade or full sun; mulch each year with leafmould. Deadhead after flowering. Propagation is by layering in autumn, or semi-ripe cuttings in late summer.

ABOVE RIGHT **This deciduous azalea is covered in late spring and early summer with clusters of sweetly fragrant flowers.**
RIGHT **The lance-shaped leaves, which act as a backdrop to the flowers in spring, come into their own in autumn.**

ROSE

Rosa moyesii

This is, without a shadow of a doubt, one of the great multiseasonal roses. *Rosa moyesii* makes a large, erect and arching shrub, of open appearance. The flowers, which appear in early summer, are single, saucer-shaped, about 5cm (2in) across, and borne at the end of short spurs. They are a deep blood-crimson, with yellow stamens. These elegant flowers are followed by extraordinary deep orange or scarlet hips, which are bulbous at the base, then narrow in the middle before widening again, much like a flask. They become evident in late summer and endure through the autumn. The leaves are neat, mid-green, and comprised of up to 13 small, oval leaflets. This deciduous shrub is suitable for growing in a group in a rose shrub border or ornamental thicket. A commonly available cultivar is *Rosa moyesii* 'Geranium', with more brightly coloured flowers.

ABOVE LEFT **The beauty and elegance of the large, single flowers is seen clearly here, in a photograph taken in early summer.**
ABOVE RIGHT **The unique red or deep orange, flask-shaped hips gradually turn brighter in colour as they decay.**

Habit: open, erect and arching
Height: up to 3m (10ft)
Spread: 1.5–2.5m (5–8ft)
Flowering season: early summer
Origin: China
Hardiness: fully hardy UK; Zone 5 US
Cultivation: this rose is very tolerant, but does best in a fertile, moisture-retentive soil, with a good organic mulch. Grow in full sun, but with shelter against winds. Minimal pruning is required. Propagate by hardwood cuttings in autumn.

EGLANTINE, SWEET BRIAR
Rosa rubiginosa

This deciduous species rose has the most charming, and evocative, common names of 'eglantine' and 'sweet briar'. The 'sweet' refers to the exquisite apple scent of the flowers and fruits, and of the leaves when crushed or after rain. It is a vigorous, healthy, very thorny species, with dark green leaves made up of five to nine, tiny, ovate leaflets. The single, cupped flowers, 2.5cm (1in) across, are a delicate rose-pink colour, with yellow centres. They appear in midsummer, and are followed by glistening and showy, ovoid, red hips, which last for months. Its arching shape and thorns make it a good subject for boundary hedging. There are a number of cultivars available from specialist nurseries, such as 'Amy Robsart' and the 'Penzance Briar' varieties.

ABOVE LEFT **The single flowers of sweet briar are carried either singly or in small clusters in midsummer.**

ABOVE RIGHT **The ovoid hips last well into winter. Not only are they brightly coloured, but they smell deliciously of apple.**

Habit: open, arching
Height: up to 2.5m (8ft)
Spread: up to 2m (6ft)
Flowering season: midsummer
Origin: Europe
Hardiness: fully hardy UK; Zone 5 US
Cultivation: like all roses, it prefers sun, in a moderately fertile soil that does not become waterlogged. That said, the sweet briar is more tolerant than many other roses. It needs little pruning in an open position, unless it has outgrown the space; however, if grown as a hedge, it should be trimmed after flowering. Propagate by hardwood cuttings in autumn.

JAPANESE ROSE
Rosa rugosa

Another excellent, multiseasonal plant, *Rosa rugosa* has dark green, narrowly oval leaves, usually made up of seven or nine leaflets. They are deciduous, deeply veined, rough and leathery to the touch (technically called 'rugose'), and turn a pleasant golden-yellow in autumn. The flowers, about 8cm (3in) across, are single and cup-shaped, with deep pink petals and a boss of yellow stamens in the centre; they resemble tissue paper as they open. They are followed by spherical, orange-red hips that resemble small tomatoes. This rose makes a very good flowering hedge, since the stems are spiny and grow densely. Recommended cultivars include 'Scabrosa', with very glossy foliage and larger purple-pink flowers, twice the size of those of the species, and 'Blanche Double de Coubert', which has semi-double scented white flowers, but does not produce hips.

Habit: upright, shrubby
Height: 1.8m (6ft)
Spread: 1.5m (5ft)
Flowering season: early summer, and then sporadically until autumn
Origin: China, Japan, Korea
Hardiness: fully hardy UK; Zone 4 US
Cultivation: this rose will tolerate light sandy soils, as well as heavier ones. It grows best in full sun. Pruning is rarely necessary, except to remove dead wood; however, if it is grown as a hedge, trim straight after the hips have started to decay. Propagation is by cuttings in autumn. The tough leaves resist pests and diseases.

ABOVE LEFT 'Scabrosa' is an excellent single cultivar of *Rosa rugosa*, with a vigorous habit, an excellent disease-resistant foliage, and lovely deep pink flowers.
LEFT In late autumn, the leaves turn yellow, forming a striking, colourful background to the tomato-like hips.

WHITE WILLOW
Salix alba subsp. *vitellina* 'Britzensis'

The white willow, *Salix alba*, makes a very imposing, large deciduous tree, much too large for most gardens. However, its subspecies 'Britzensis' can be cut back hard, to take advantage of the brightly coloured, orange-yellow young stems in winter. This should be done every year, in spring, once one or several stems have reached about 2m (6ft) high, and after the showy yellow catkins have flowered.

The leaves are lance-shaped, green on the upper sides and blue-green beneath. The best effects can be achieved if this plant is grown in association with, e.g., *S. acutifolia* 'Blue Streak', *S. alba* 'Chermesina', *S. daphnoides*, *S. irrorata*, and with other barked trees such as *Acer capillipes* and *A. griseum*. These plants combine to create a varied display of stem and bark colour.

ABOVE LEFT **The green leaves, present on the tree from spring to autumn, lighten in colour before they fall.**

ABOVE RIGHT **The warmly glowing, orange-yellow stems enliven even the dullest of winter days. To retain the bright colour, the stems should be cut back every spring.**

Habit: pollarded
Height: 2m (6ft), when pollarded
Spread: up to 3m (10ft)
Flowering season: late winter to early spring
Origin of species: Europe, north Africa, central Asia
Hardiness: fully hardy UK; Zone 3 US
Cultivation: plant in moist, fertile soil in sun. If the soil is shrinkable clay, plant a considerable distance from drains or foundations: the roots, even of pollarded willows, are far-reaching. Propagation is by hardwood cuttings in winter.

JAPANESE SKIMMIA
Skimmia japonica

Skimmia japonica is not a plant to set the pulses racing, but it can provide useful, and colourful, evergreen groundcover, even in shade or coastal areas. It makes a rounded, dense shrub, usually no more than 90cm (36in) tall (although it can get taller with age), with thick, oval or lance-shaped, pale green, glossy leaves, up to 10cm (4in) long. The scented flowers appear in spring and are small, white or off-white, star-shaped and held in dense panicles. Among the clones of *Skimmia japonica* are both male and female plants; the female is the berrying kind, but requires a male nearby for cross-fertilization. In the female clone 'Nymans', the spherical berries are especially large and freely produced. There is a good male clone, 'Rubella', which has red-edged leaves and red flower buds. Skimmias do best in woodland or a partially shaded shrubbery.

ABOVE LEFT **In winter, the female form of *Skimmia japonica* produces spherical, bright red fruits, but only if there are male plants in close proximity.**
ABOVE RIGHT **Scented white flowers adorn this plant in spring. Provided the soil is fertile and moist, skimmias will thrive even in an alkaline soil.**

Habit: low, dome-shaped or creeping
Height: up to 1.2m (4ft)
Spread: up to 2m (6ft)
Flowering season: spring
Origin: China, Japan
Hardiness: fully hardy UK; Zone 7 US
Cultivation: it thrives in a fertile, moist but well-drained soil, and may become cholorotic in a poor, alkaline soil. Male and female flowers are borne on different plants, so grow them in groups of about one male to five females, for good berrying. Root semi-ripe cuttings in summer.

Spiraea thunbergii

This is an underrated shrub that finds a place here because it combines an attractive habit, pretty flowers in early to mid-spring, and striking autumn colour. Its virtues also include amenability and reliability. It is small to medium sized, with a bushy habit, and narrow, pointed, smooth, green, deciduous or semi-evergreen leaves that turn deep red and orange in autumn. The saucer-shaped flowers are pure white, and held in many small clusters, up to 5cm (2in) across, close to the arching shoots; indeed, it is so floriferous that the twigs are hidden completely. *Spirea thunbergii* is the first spiraea to flower. It combines well with other shrubs, or with spring-flowering bulbs. The sprays of flowers are good for cutting. Similar garden-worthy spiraeas include *S.* 'Arguta' (the spring-flowering bridal wreath spiraea) and *S.* x *vanhouttei* (which flowers in early summer).

Habit: dense, with arching shoots
Height: up to 1.5m (5ft)
Spread: up to 2m (6ft)
Flowering season: late spring
Origin: China, Japan
Hardiness: hardy UK, but the flowers may be damaged by a late frost; Zone 5 US
Cultivation: grow in any reasonably fertile soil, in full sun. If the shrub becomes straggly, prune it back hard straight after flowering. Propagate by semi-ripe cuttings in summer.

ABOVE RIGHT **In late spring, this dense shrub is covered in small, pure-white, saucer-shaped flowers.**
RIGHT **The leaves gradually change from mid-green in summer to orange, yellow and red in autumn.**

FALSE CAMELLIA
Stewartia pseudocamellia

Although strictly speaking a deciduous tree, this stewartia finds a place here because it is slow-growing, rarely reaches anything like 20m (70ft), and is usually planted with shrubs in a woodland setting. It has exquisite flowers carried for several weeks in midsummer, leaves that colour well in autumn, and intriguing, flaking red-brown bark, which is an attractive feature in winter. The long-lasting, camellia-like flowers, 6cm (2½in) across, are cup-shaped with five white petals, and a central boss of yellow stamens; they are borne singly or in pairs. At the end of the season, the whole flower drops, rather than just the petals. The false camellia bears fruit, but it is not very showy. The leaves are oval, tapered at the tip and toothed, and are matt-green on the upper sides but glossy-green beneath. This plant thrives in acid woodland, and will associate well with rhododendrons and other ericaceous plants. There is another, similar species sometimes encountered, called *Stewartia sinensis*, which has even brighter leaf colour in autumn, and fragrant white flowers.

ABOVE LEFT **These large, pure-white flowers really do resemble those of single camellias, hence this plant's common name.**

ABOVE RIGHT **A mature plant is a fine sight, even in winter when there is no foliage. The red-brown bark flakes away to reveal a pinkish grey trunk beneath.**

Habit: Broadly columnar, open
Height: up to 20m (70ft)
Spread: up to 7m (22ft)
Flowering season: midsummer
Origin: Japan
Hardiness: fully hardy UK; Zone 6 US
Cultivation: grow in light shade, or full sun, in a sheltered place, and in fertile, moist but free-draining, neutral or acid soil. Pruning is usually unnecessary. Propagation is by layering or sowing seeds in autumn, or semi-ripe cuttings in late summer.

Viburnum × juddii

Viburnum, like *Malus*, is without exception an excellent genus. All viburnums are garden worthy, and perform in two seasons or more. The small to medium-sized deciduous shrub, *Viburnum × juddii*, is one of the real stars, because it flowers freely in mid-spring, after most of the flowering bulbs have finished, and before the summer shrubs have come into their own. Its round heads of sturdy, yet dainty, flowers exude a strong and delicious scent, giving a hint as to its parentage (*V. bitchiuense* × *V. carlesii*). The flowers have pink tubes, which open out into white stars; the clusters can cover a bush. The leaves are neat, oval, and dark green, and turn red in autumn. This shrub can be clipped to form a hedge or specimen.

Habit: rounded, densely branched
Height: 1.5m (5ft)
Spread: 1.5m (5ft)
Flowering season: mid- to late spring
Origin: garden origin
Hardiness: fully hardy UK; Zone 5 US
Cultivation: viburnums thrive in a fertile, moist but well-drained soil, but they are not fussy, and like alkalinity. They flower best in sun, but also tolerate partial shade. Prune after flowering. Propagate by softwood cuttings in summer.

ABOVE RIGHT **The flowers are not long lived, but come at an opportune time in mid-spring and are highly fragrant.**
RIGHT **This neat, versatile shrub (shown here in autumn) deserves a prominent place; it offers many features of interest, and makes an excellent specimen or hedge.**

GUELDER ROSE
Viburnum opulus 'Xanthocarpum'

The guelder rose, *Viburnum opulus*, is a must for every garden, because of its lovely flowers in summer, long-lasting berries and excellent autumn colour. The flat flower heads, 8cm (3in) across, are much like those of a lacecap hydrangea, and are composed of tubular, creamy white, fertile flowers in the centre, surrounded by showy white, sterile florets. The fruit, which resembles a redcurrant, is round and fleshy, and carried in bunches. The deciduous leaves are five-lobed, like a maple, dark green, and often turn glorious shades of orange

and red in autumn. There are a number of cultivars, all garden worthy: 'Xanthocarpum' is a medium-sized, multi-stemmed shrub, with bright yellow fruit, which becomes translucent as it ripens, but is otherwise identical. This viburnum can be grown as a specimen, but produces the most profuse berries when planted in small groups. Other excellent varieties of the guelder rose include 'Notcutt's Variety', which has larger flowers and fruit than the normal one; and 'Compactum', which would be a good choice for a small garden.

ABOVE LEFT **The ornamental flower heads, consisting of tiny creamy white and white flowers, are striking set against the dark green, maple-like leaves.**
ABOVE RIGHT **These translucent, bright yellow fruits are the shrub's glory in early and mid-autumn.**

Habit: bushy, spreading
Height: up to 5m (15ft)
Spread: up to 4m (12ft)
Flowering season: early summer
Origin of species: Europe, north Africa, Asia
Hardiness: fully hardy UK; Zone 3 US
Cultivation: this plant thrives in very moist, even boggy conditions, but is happy in a variety of soil types. It likes sun or partial shade. Trim lightly after flowering, or remove some stems in early spring to lessen overcrowding. Propagation is by softwood cuttings in summer.

JAPANESE SNOWBALL TREE
Viburnum plicatum 'Mariesii'

This is a deciduous shrub for a prominent place in the garden, where it can be seen easily at all times of the year. Its great merits are its habit, its spectacular flowers, and its neat foliage, which usually colours well in autumn; indeed, its only shortcoming, if it can be called that, is that it does not produce berries freely, as so many other viburnums do.

As the shrub matures, its branches become horizontal and tiered, a most unusual feature in a shrub, and unknown otherwise among viburnums. The cymes of flowers are long lasting and very striking: they are about 8cm (3in) across, and appear in late spring and remain until early summer. They consist of many creamy white flowers, surrounded by flat, sterile, pure-white florets. The leaves, up to 10cm (4in) long, are heart-shaped and tapered, mid- to dark green, and deeply veined; they turn red-purple in autumn. This plant is ideal as a specimen in a lawn or shrubbery.

Habit: rounded, tiered
Height: up to 3m (10ft)
Spread: 2–3m (6–10ft)
Flowering season: late spring and early summer
Origin: garden origin
Hardiness: fully hardy UK; Zone 5 US
Cultivation: viburnums like alkaline soil and, although not fussy, they thrive in a fertile, moist but well-drained soil. They flower better in full sun, but are also happy in partial shade. Propagate by softwood or semi-ripe cuttings in summer.

ABOVE RIGHT **The flowers draw the eye in summer, but the exceptional feature of this mature shrub is its tiered habit, which is striking even in winter.**
RIGHT **A second crop of flowers in autumn is a not uncommon and welcome bonus to the reliable autumn leaf colour.**

CLIMBERS
AND WALL SHRUBS

Climbers and wall shrubs play an important role in the garden's evolving seasonal progress. Gardeners delight in their flowers and fruit and exploit their vigour to rapidly clothe walls and pergolas. Since climbing plants do not take up valuable ground space, they are particularly useful in smaller gardens.

BELOW **The ideal wall plant, *Cotoneaster horizontalis*, is here seen in mid-winter. It will thrive in a poor soil and needs little or no training.**

JAPANESE QUINCE
Chaenomeles x *superba* 'Crimson and Gold'

Japanese quinces form a group of plants that can be used either as specimen shrubs or, more usually, trained against a wall. *C.* x *superba* (a cross between *C. japonica* and *C. speciosa*) is the best hybrid, and there are a number of good selections, including the very striking 'Crimson and Gold'. The leaves are smallish, oval, glossy green, finely toothed, and borne on spiny branches. The flowers, in clusters, appear before and after the leaves emerge; they are cup-shaped, 4cm (1½in) across, dark red in colour, with prominent golden stamens (hence the common name). The fruit is aromatic and yellowish green, and resembles a small quince; it is edible, if cooked. Other good cultivars include 'Knap Hill Scarlet', orange-scarlet; 'Pink Lady', with large, dark pink, early flowers; and 'Rowallane', with bright crimson flowers.

Habit: spreading
Height: 1–1.5m (3–5ft)
Spread: 2m (6ft)
Flowering season: spring to early summer
Origin: garden origin
Hardiness: fully hardy UK; Zone 5 US
Cultivation: plant against a sunny or partially shaded wall in well-drained, ordinary soil. Regularly remove branches growing away from the wall. After flowering, trim back flowered shoots, to within four buds of the framework, so as to retain the fruit, and cut away a few older branches, to retain the plant's vigour. Propagate by semi-ripe cuttings in summer.

ABOVE LEFT **The rich red and golden-yellow flowers can add a vibrant splash of colour to a featureless wall in spring.**
ABOVE RIGHT **The fragrant yellow fruit, which ripens in autumn, can be cooked and made into jam or jelly.**
RIGHT **This shrub grows best trained against a wall since it flowers so early. It will need pruning and tying in.**

DOWNY CLEMATIS
Clematis 'Rosie O'Grady'

Clematis macropetala has four long petals and four shorter, petal-like stamens inside. Within these are yellow stamens. The flowers are about 10cm (4in) across, violet-blue and, in the case of 'Rosie O'Grady', a pinkish mauve. They come out in spring, and continue until early summer, with occasionally a second flowering, and are followed by silky silver seedheads, which become fluffy as they age. The leaves are mid-green in colour, and made up of nine oval leaflets. This is not a strong-growing plant, which makes it ideal for climbing up a fence, over a tree stump or through a large, sturdy shrub. There are several good *C. macropetala* cultivars; others to look out for are 'Maidwell Hall', with deep blue flowers and 'White Swan', compact and with white flowers.

Habit: scrambling, climbing by leaf stalks
Height: up to 2.5m (8ft)
Spread: up to 2m (6ft)
Flowering season: mid-spring to summer
Origin of species: China, Mongolia, Russia
Hardiness: fully hardy UK; Zone 5 US
Cultivation: *C. macropetala* and its cultivars will grow on a north-facing wall or fence, although they thrive best where there is more sun and their roots are shaded. A fertile, humus-rich soil suits clematis best, together with a mulch in late winter. *C. macropetala* does not need much pruning, just the removal of dead wood and over-long shoots after flowering. Layer *in situ* in winter or in early spring.

ABOVE LEFT **The four long petals and four shorter petals inside give this clematis the appearance of having semi-double flowers.**
LEFT **The seedheads are at their most silky and alluring in late summer. They become fluffy and greyish as they age.**

LEMON PEEL CLEMATIS
Clematis tangutica

Midsummer to autumn can be a barren time for climbing plants, so the pretty, long-lasting, late-season flowers of *Clematis tangutica* are usually much appreciated. These grow abundantly and are yellow, nodding and lantern-shaped, about 5cm (2in) long, with thick petals that bear a passing resemblance to lemon peel (hence the common name). The flowers are followed by silky seedheads. The leaves are deciduous, bright green and delicately divided. The species can be variable, so it is best to grow a good cultivar, such as 'Aureolin', with larger flowers, or 'Lambton Park', which comes into flower in early summer. *Clematis tangutica* and its cultivars will scramble over a bank or tree stump, or will grow against a wall, trellis or fence.

ABOVE LEFT **The remarkably thick petals of this clematis resemble lemon peel, hence the common name.**
ABOVE RIGHT **The silky seedheads are a delight, and can last for several months in good condition.**

Habit: scrambling, climbing by leaf stalks
Height: up to 5m (15ft)
Spread: 2m (6ft)
Flowering season: midsummer to late autumn, depending on severity of pruning (*see below*)
Origin: central Asia, western China
Hardiness: fully hardy UK; Zone 5 US
Cultivation: these clematis thrive in a moist, fertile, not-too-acid soil. Mulch well in early spring, and water in dry weather. Prune back hard in late winter, but more lightly if you want early flowers. Layer in winter or early spring.

FISHBONE COTONEASTER
Cotoneaster horizontalis

Although very commonly grown, the so-called fishbone cotoneaster should never be discounted. Not only is it reliable and amenable, but it is good looking and distinctive as well. It can be grown either against a wall – where the herringbone tracery of the somewhat flattened branches may be seen to best advantage – or as a free-standing, rather prostrate shrub. The tiny leaves, up to 1cm (½in) long, are neat and held close to the branches. They emerge in spring, initially furled inwards, and turn bright red reliably in autumn before they fall. The flowers, carried singly or in pairs, are white, sometimes tinged with pink, and borne in quantity in late spring. They are much loved by bees. The berries are small, orange-red and popular with birds; how long they last in autumn depends on the availability of other food sources. This is one of the first choices for brightening up a shady wall or a difficult bank. 'Variegatus' is an attractive variegated cultivar, with cream edges to the leaves.

ABOVE LEFT **A mature fishbone cotoneaster, grown against a shaded wall, is a fine sight.**
ABOVE RIGHT **The leaves may only be 1cm (½in) long but, in quantity, are a superb sight in autumn before they fall.**

Habit: prostrate, or vertical against a wall
Height: up to 90cm (36in)
Spread: up to 1.8m (6ft)
Flowering season: late spring
Origin: China
Hardiness: fully hardy UK; Zone 5 US
Cultivation: this plant will grow in any soil and can withstand drought. No pruning is normally required. Sow seed in autumn, or take cuttings in early summer.

CLIMBING HYDRANGEA
Hydrangea anomala subsp. *petiolaris*

Usually sold as *Hydrangea petiolaris*, this climbing hydrangea, which produces aerial roots by which it clings to its host, enjoys deserved popularity because it will grow on a north- or east-facing wall, and requires neither tying in nor, usually, pruning. It will also cling to the trunk of a tall tree. It is deciduous, so there is the interest of its heart-shaped, serrated, dark green leaves unfurling in spring, as well as excellent yellow autumn colour. But the real glory of this plant resides in the rounded heads of creamy white flowers, up to 25cm (10in) across, consisting of fertile florets surrounded by a ring of flat sterile ones. These appear in early summer. The trunk also has a flaky bark.

Habit: climbing, self-clinging
Height: 5–15m (16–50ft)
Spread: indeterminate
Flowering season: early summer
Origin: Japan, Korea, Sakhalin, Taiwan
Hardiness: fully hardy UK; Zone 5 US
Cultivation: grow in reasonably fertile, but well-drained soil, in partial shade, and keep from drought in summer. This climber is slow to get going, initially. Pruning is not required, unless it outgrows its space. Propagate by taking softwood cuttings in summer, or hardwood cuttings in winter.

ABOVE RIGHT **The creamy white flowers in rounded clusters last for many weeks in summer.**

RIGHT **The leaves gradually turn butter-yellow before falling and revealing the flaky bark beneath.**

CHINESE VIRGINIA CREEPER
Parthenocissus henryana
(syn. *Ampelopsis henryana*)

There is much confusion about the common name of this useful and vigorous creeper. It is often called, loosely, 'Virginia creeper', but that honour really goes to *P. quinquefolia*. *P. henryana* is properly, and paradoxically, called the 'Chinese Virginia creeper'. It makes an excellent wall plant, because it climbs by means of tiny, disc-shaped suckers which attach themselves to hard surfaces; as a result, no tying-in is needed. The distinctive leaves are shaped like an outstretched hand, and composed of five leaflets, which are attached only at the base. These leaflets are large, oval and coarsely toothed. They are green, with very striking silver or silvery pink veins on the upper sides, and purple beneath, and turn a fiery scarlet in the autumn. The flowers in early summer are insignificant. The Chinese Virginia creeper makes a very fine clothing to a tall house, especially one made of pale-coloured brick or stone, for the autumn colour of the leaves will clash with red brick. Other good species include *P. quinquefolia*, which also has brilliant red leaves before they fall, and Boston ivy (*P. tricuspidata*), which turns red to purple in autumn.

ABOVE LEFT **This self-clinging climber is an excellent choice for a large house but is unsuitable elsewhere.**
ABOVE RIGHT **The venation, so prominent in spring, gradually loses definition as the leaves change colour in autumn.**

Habit: climbing, self-clinging
Height: up to 30m (100ft), but usually about 8–10m (25–30ft)
Spread: about 5m (15ft)
Flowering season: early summer
Origin: China
Hardiness: frost hardy UK; Zone 7 US
Cultivation: plant in good soil in a partially-shaded spot. In early winter, and often also in late summer, cut back shoots to fit the area required. Cuttings can be taken from early summer to winter.

PASSION FLOWER
Passiflora caerulea

The passion flower can be capricious in flowering and fruiting but, if planted where it will thrive, is a valuable and striking wall plant. The flowers are fascinating and highly intricate, consisting of ten greenish white, pink-tinged petals, surrounding rows of thin, purple, blue and white filaments, which make up the 'corona'. These, in turn, surround five stamens and three styles, which protrude. The common name relates to the fact that missionaries in Central and South America used the flowers of this genus to explain Christ's Passion. The fruit is egg-shaped, orange-yellow, up to 6cm (2½in) long, and edible; it ripens in autumn, although not reliably when grown in cooler climates. The evergreen or semi-evergreen leaves are large, bright green, divided into usually five lobes, and carried on grooved stems. The stems also produce spiralling tendrils, by which the plant clings to its support.

Habit: climbing by tendrils
Height: up to 10m (30ft), but less in cool climates
Spread: indeterminate
Flowering season: all through the summer
Origin: South America
Hardiness: frost hardy UK; Zone 7 US
Cultivation: plant against a warm, sheltered wall, in free-draining soil. It may be cut back by winter frosts, but is seldom killed. (It can also be grown in a cool conservatory.) In early spring, cut back sideshoots to 3 or 4 buds from main framework. Propagate by semi-ripe cuttings in summer.

ABOVE RIGHT **The fascinating flowers of** *Passiflora caerulea* **reward close observation.**
RIGHT **The fruits of the passion flower are edible, but do not ripen in cooler climates.**

FIRETHORN
Pyracantha 'Orange Glow'

The genus *Pyracantha* contains many suitable subjects for multiseasonal planting; they have long been popular for their evergreen leaves, their profuse flowers and, above all, their showy clusters of yellow, orange or red berries. Pyracanthas can be grown as free-standing shrubs, trained against walls, or as hedges. They have thorny branches.

Pyracantha 'Orange Glow' is a well-known cultivar, with glossy, dark green, toothed, oblong leaves, up to 5cm (2in) long, and, in early summer, clusters of small white flowers, similar to those of hawthorn (*Crataegus*), followed by masses of deep orange berries. These are long lasting, provided they are not eaten by birds. This cultivar is resistant to pyracantha scab. Other cultivars, all of which flower in early summer, include 'Navaho', with flattened orange-red berries; 'Shawnee', with slightly flattened orange-yellow berries; and 'Teton', with masses of yellow-orange berries. These have shown some resistance to diseases, such as pyracantha scab and fireblight.

Habit: upright and spreading
Height: up to 3m (10ft)
Spread: up to 3m (10ft)
Flowering season: early summer
Origin: garden origin
Hardiness: fully hardy UK; Zone 6 US
Cultivation: pyracanthas do best in full sun or light shade, in a fertile, well-drained soil. If wall trained, shorten the sideshoots after flowering, and remove unwanted outward-facing shoots. Those in the open need little pruning. Hedges should be trimmed just after flowering. Take semi-ripe cuttings in summer.

ABOVE LEFT **This shrub is extremely generous in its flowering and fruiting.**
LEFT **The berries, in particular, are long lasting. It is a shrub that will grow in the open, but looks best against a wall, as here.**

GRAPE VINE
Vitis vinifera 'Purpurea'

The purple-leaved grape vine makes a very fine plant for a large wall, trellis, fence or pergola. It combines lovely silver-downed young shoots with handsome purple foliage during the summer, and signs off with wonderful autumn colour. To these attributes is added ornamental purple grapes.

The so-called 'Teinturier grape' climbs by means of tendrils that twine around the support. The stems become woody with age. It has large, three-lobed leaves, 15cm (6in) across, with very coarse serrations. These are silvery purple when young, becoming purple with age, then bright red and crimson in autumn. The flowers are small, and borne in clusters in late spring, then followed in autumn by lush, deep purple round grapes, with a blue bloom to them. Unfortunately, these grapes are not palatable.

ABOVE LEFT **The bloom on the fruit is extremely attractive set against the leaves turning to scarlet in early autumn.**
ABOVE RIGHT **The young shoots are covered in downy hairs, which make them look silver.**

Habit: climbing by tendrils
Height: up to 9m (28ft)
Spread: indeterminate
Flowering season: late spring
Origin of species: Europe
Hardiness: fully hardy UK; Zone 6 US
Cultivation: plant in fertile, well-drained but moisture-retentive, neutral or alkaline soil. It prefers full sun, but will tolerate some shade. Trim back shoots in winter if it is outgrowing its space. Layer in autumn, or take hardwood cuttings in winter.

BORDER PLANTS

While trees and shrubs provide the setting and backdrop to the garden stage, border plants, such as perennials, annuals and flowering bulbs, are the fast-moving entertainers who add excitement, variation and a fascinating, ever-changing kaleidoscope of shape and colour.

BELOW **The flowers of the peony, *Paeonia mlokosewitchii*, are only one of its attributes; it also has leaves which colour in both spring and autumn.**

YARROW
Achillea 'Moonshine'

Ornamental yarrows have for a long time enjoyed a prominent place in our gardens, because of their reliability and their long-lasting flowers. Today, these perennials are available in a wider range of colours, from white through pink to yellow and deep red, which makes them even more attractive to gardeners. Most yarrows have attractive, ferny foliage, which looks especially good in spring.

One of the best of the long-established *Achillea* is the hybrid 'Moonshine', because it combines persistent foliage, which is an attractive silvery green, with clear yellow flowers.

These daisy-type flowers, popular with butterflies and bees, are individually very small, but held in flat flower heads, up to 15cm (6in) across. The flower heads can be depended upon to remain colourful and fresh for several months, from early summer to early autumn; they then develop seedheads, which persist until spring. They make very good subjects for drying for indoor decoration. Other excellent cultivars include *A. filipendulina* 'Gold Plate', with bright golden flowers; *A.* 'Lachsschönheit', with salmon-pink flowers; and *A.* 'Summerwine', with dark red, white-centred flowers.

ABOVE LEFT **The foliage, which persists through the winter, is a splendid foil for colourful perennials.**

ABOVE RIGHT **Its clean colour and long lasting flowers means 'Moonshine' associates well with perennials, such as *Alchemilla mollis*, and sub-shrubs, such as *Santolina pinnata neapolitana* and *Cistus*.**

Habit: clump-forming, erect
Height: 60cm (24in)
Spread: up to 60cm (24in)
Flowering season: early summer to early autumn
Origin: garden origin
Hardiness: fully hardy UK; Zone 3 US
Cultivation: it will thrive in a moist but well-drained soil in full sun, but will tolerate less than ideal conditions. Divide frequently in spring to keep it flowering well.

ORNAMENTAL ONION
Allium cristophii
(syn. *A. albopilosum*)

Most bulbous plants have only one season of interest, even if it is often a spectacular one. Some of the ornamental onions, however, earn their keep twice over: they have very striking flowers, and their seedheads are unique. One of the best, and most widely available, is *Allium cristophii* (syn. *A. albopilosum*). This has large, spherical flower heads, about 20cm (8in) across, carried on ribbed stems up to 60cm (24in) tall; these heads are made up of many small, star-shaped, silvery purple flowers. After they go over, the black seedheads develop. The flower heads can be left in the garden over winter, or cut and dried for indoor decoration. The leaves are short lived, dying off before the flowers appear in early summer. They are strap-shaped, hairy, and grey-green in colour, and white underneath. This is a plant to grow in a group for the best effect. *A. schubertii* has even larger heads, but is harder to find commercially. There are ornamental onions with smaller flower heads, which nevertheless make an impact in a sunny border because the flowers are so densely packed. A popular species is the purple *A. hollandicum* (syn. *A. aflatunense*).

ABOVE LEFT **With its large, spherical flower heads on tall, leafless stems, this allium is prized for its striking architectural habit.**
ABOVE RIGHT **A must for flower arrangers, the heads of this allium dry very well.**

Habit: erect
Height: about 60cm (24in)
Spread: 20cm (8in)
Flowering season: early summer
Origin: Iran, Turkey
Hardiness: frost hardy UK; Zone 4 US
Cultivation: alliums are best planted in a very well-drained soil, in full sun, about 10cm (4in) deep, in autumn. To propagate bulbous species, such as *A. cristophii*, remove offsets and replant in autumn.

BLUE STAR
Amsonia tabernaemontana

A well-behaved herbaceous perennial, *Amsonia tabernaemontana* has charming flowers and good, long-lasting autumn leaf colour. It makes a neat clump, about 80cm (32in) tall when flowering, with small, willow-like leaves in whorls up the stems, and pale blue, star-shaped, five-petalled flowers in pyramidal heads at the end of them. It starts flowering in late spring, and continues through to midsummer. In autumn, the leaves turn to a light, glowing yellow.

  Amsonia tabernaemontana will thrive even in damp partial shade. In flower, it associates well with peonies, irises, geraniums and other early summer-flowering plants; when the leaves have turned, it combines well with grasses, autumn-flowering chrysanthemums and other flowers in the daisy family (*Compositae*). The flowers can be picked for indoor decoration, but if the stems are broken, they exude a milky sap that can irritate the skin.

Habit: clump-forming, erect
Height: 80cm–100cm (32–39in)
Spread: 45cm (18in)
Flowering season: late spring to midsummer
Origin: eastern USA
Hardiness: fully hardy UK; Zone 3 US
Cultivation: plant in a moist, fertile soil in full sun or partial shade. It will stand a certain amount of short-lived drought. Propagate by division in spring, softwood cuttings in summer, or sow seed in autumn or spring.

ABOVE RIGHT **The pale, sky-blue flowers are up to 2cm (¾in) across, and held in clusters.**
RIGHT **The autumn leaf colour is long lasting, and associates well with autumn-flowering perennials, such as hardy chrysanthemums.**

WHITE MUGWORT
Artemisia lactiflora 'Guizhou'

The perennial *Artemisia lactiflora* is an unusual member of the genus, since it thrives in moist soil, and because it has flowers that actually enhance the plant. It grows to about 1.5m (5ft) when flowering in late summer and early autumn. The leaves are jagged and dark green, and up to 25cm (10in) long. The small, creamy white flowers are held in open panicles, which last well and can be cut and dried for indoor use as decoration. 'Guizhou' is a more elegant cultivar, with attractive purple stems and young leaves, and more widely spreading flower heads. It is quite adaptable and can be used in a sunny border, at the edge of woodlands, or in the light shade cast by small trees. It makes a good companion for pink Japanese anemones (*A.* x *hybrida*), pink opium poppies (*Papaver somniferum*), astilbes, blue asters and glaucous-leaved hostas.

ABOVE LEFT **What distinguishes 'Guizhou' from the ordinary white mugwort are the purple young leaves and stems.**
ABOVE RIGHT **By the time this white mugwort flowers in late summer, it has reached 1.5m (5ft) tall and has become an imposing plant.**

Habit: clump-forming, erect
Height: up to 1.5m (5ft)
Spread: 60cm (24in)
Flowering season: late summer and early autumn
Origin of species: western China
Hardiness: fully hardy UK; Zone 4 US
Cultivation: this artemisia is best grown in a fertile, moisture-retentive soil in full sun or light shade. It may well need staking. Propagate by division, or by semi-ripe, heeled cuttings in early summer.

ELEPHANT'S EARS
Bergenia 'Sunningdale'

Bergenias, or 'elephant's ears' as they are known colloquially, are enormously welcome in the garden, because they belong to that select band of perennials that are evergreen. Thus they give colour and life to a flower border, even in the depths of winter. 'Sunningdale' is a particularly good cultivar, having large, rounded leaves, which are red below and mid-green above in the summer, but take on attractive bronze-red tones in winter. Moreover, it has some of the most striking flowers of the genus: these are deep magenta-pink, and held in clusters at the top of relatively tall, red stems, up to 45cm (18in) high. They last for a long period in spring.

Bergenias make good edging or weed-smothering groundcover in spacious surroundings, and their tolerance of poor soil and shade endears them to all gardeners. Other good bergenias for winter colour are *B.* 'Abendglut' and *B. purpurascens*. Bergenias are often placed with other winter- and early-spring flowerers with imposing foliage, such as the Lenten rose (*Helleborus orientalis*).

Habit: clump-forming groundcover
Height: up to 45cm (18in)
Spread: up to 60cm (24in)
Flowering season: early and mid-spring
Origin: garden origin
Hardiness: hardy UK, although flowers may be damaged by hard frosts; Zone 4 US.
Cultivation: this plant will grow lushly in a fertile, moist soil in sun or partial shade, but winter colour is best where temperatures are low or the soil is impoverished. Do not plant too close to the front of a border, unless there is paved edging, since the leaves will kill the grass of a lawn. Propagate by division in autumn or spring.

ABOVE RIGHT **This is one of the best bergenias for flowers: they are deep magenta-pink, and appear in early spring.**
RIGHT **The best autumn and winter colour occurs if the soil is poor, the temperatures low and the leaves in full sun.**

Cyclamen hederifolium

Of all the hardy cyclamen, *C. hederifolium* is the best known, and deservedly so. It has two marked seasons of interest. In late summer and autumn, from an underground tuber, it sends up a succession of enchanting flowers; these are followed (although sometimes there is an overlap) by unusual and decorative leaves, which persist through the winter and die down only for the midsummer months. The flower consists of a corolla, with the petals twisted slightly and bent right back; it is usually pale pink with a maroon mouth, but there is also a well-known white form called var. *hederifolium* f. *albiflorum*. The leaves are reasonably large, heart-shaped or triangular, purple beneath and grey-green, with distinctive patterns picked out in silver, cream and grey, on top. These leaves act as effective groundcover for the six or seven months that they are on display.

ABOVE LEFT **No two leaves of cyclamen are ever quite the same. They appear after the flowering has started.**

ABOVE RIGHT **The mixture of white and pink cyclamens is winning; you should allow the colony to self-seed and spread if possible.**

Habit: ground-covering
Height: up to 12cm (5in)
Spread: up to 15cm (6in)
Flowering season: late summer and early autumn
Origin: southern Europe
Hardiness: fully hardy UK; Zone 5 US
Cultivation: plant 5cm (2in) deep in a humus-rich soil, in partial shade. Lightly mulch with leafmould in summer. Sow seed when ripe, having soaked it first.

CARDOON
Cynara cardunculus

The herbaceous perennial *Cynara cardunculus* is a member of the thistle family, and is a sensational addition to the large flower border, because of its enormous size and the sculptural quality of its leaves and flower heads. It is sometimes confused with one of the globe artichokes, *Cynara scolymus*, but cardoons have more finely cut leaves and smaller, but more numerous, flower heads. These are edible only if the young leaf stalks and midribs are grown, covered in cardboard to blanch them, and then cooked.

The backward-arching leaves have deeply cut opposite lobes, are silver-grey in colour, very spiny, and up to 90cm (36in) long. The flowers, carried on furry stems from summer to early autumn, are purple thistles, prickly, and up to 8cm (3in) in diameter. They are much prized by flower arrangers (if picked before opening, and put in water to expand). The flowers can also be dried for winter decoration.

Habit: sculptural, clump-forming
Height: up to 2.4m (8ft)
Spread: about 1.2–1.5m (4–5ft)
Flowering season: high summer to early autumn
Origin: Mediterranean region
Hardiness: fully hardy UK; Zone 7 US
Cultivation: grow cardoons in a fertile, well-drained soil, in a sheltered sunny place. If you want particularly silvery leaves, remove the flower stems as they appear. In cold areas, cover the crown with a mulch to avoid frost penetration. Plants may be divided in late spring, or take root cuttings in winter.

ABOVE RIGHT **The leaves are quick to grow in spring, and remain fresh for longer if the flower stems are removed.**
RIGHT **The flowers are held at the top of 2m (6ft) stems from summer to early autumn.**

UMBRELLA PLANT
Darmera peltata (syn. *Peltiphyllum peltatum*)

This is a most striking perennial for the waterside, grown for its flowers and enormous, umbrella-like leaves. In early spring, before the leaves appear, tall, naked, hairy stems swiftly elongate, carrying flattened heads, 12cm (5in) across, of many five-petalled, white or pink flowers. After the flowers, the leaves emerge, borne on stalks 1m (3ft) high; they are dark green, rounded, toothed, lobed, and heavily veined. They grow up to 60cm (24in) across, making this a most imposing plant, almost in the same league as *Gunnera manicata*, but hardier. They also gradually turn a pleasing bronze-red in autumn. This plant has rhizomes, which slowly spread and colonize. There is also a dwarf form, 'Nana', whose leaves grow only to 30cm (12in) high and 25cm (10in) across. This plant gives a good sense of massiveness to the edge of a small pond.

ABOVE LEFT **These flowers on naked stems have a striking impact at the edge of a stream or pond in early spring.**
ABOVE RIGHT **As the flowers fade, the large 'elephant's hoof' leaves expand, providing excellent summer groundcover.**

Habit: mound-forming
Height: 2m (6ft)
Spread: 90cm (36in) or more
Flowering season: early spring
Origin: Pacific Coast, USA
Hardiness: fully hardy UK; Zone 6 US
Cultivation: this plant will grow in sun or shade. It requires a very moist situation, with a deep soil, a waterside spot being ideal. The soil should not dry out in summer. To propagate, divide rhizomes in spring.

PINK
Dianthus 'Doris'

Dianthus is the generic name for carnations and pinks, and all could find a place in this book, because they combine neat, steely blue evergreen foliage with lovely fragrant flowers. Some of the best for garden use are the group called 'modern pinks', since they are fully hardy, vigorous, need little attention and may be cut for indoor decoration. They usually bloom more than once, particularly if the dying flowers are removed regularly.

'Doris' is one of the best loved of the modern pinks. It has linear, pointed, blue-grey leaves, which make a compact, ground-covering mound. The flowers, up to 6cm (2½in) across, and carried in groups of four to six on a stem, are scented, double, and bi-coloured, that is pale pink on the outer edge of the flower and darker, more salmon-pink or sometimes scarlet in the centre. They begin to flower in early summer, and produce several flushes until autumn. 'Doris' goes well with warm pink roses and oriental poppies (*Papaver orientale*), such as 'Mrs Perry', and will associate with a wide variety of plants. Other good modern pink cultivars (all with double scented flowers) include 'Gran's Favourite', white with pink-mauve centres and edges; 'Haytor White', pure white; and 'Widecombe Fair', with pale apricot flowers.

ABOVE LEFT **The neat evergreen foliage of this mat-forming pink is an ideal edging, or foil for hot colours when not in flower.**
ABOVE RIGHT **'Doris' and other 'modern pinks' produce several flushes of flowers through the summer.**

Habit: compact, mound-forming
Height: up to 30cm (12in)
Spread: about 40cm (16in)
Flowering season: early summer to autumn
Origin: garden origin
Hardiness: fully hardy UK; Zone 4 US
Cultivation: grow modern pinks in well-drained soil, which is not very acid, in full sun. Deadhead regularly. Take softwood cuttings in summer.

BURNING BUSH, DITTANY
Dictamnus albus
var. *purpureus*

This woody-based perennial produces decorative and distinctive flowers in early summer, before the main mass of hardy perennials. Its common name derives from the fact that it gives off an oil which, on hot still evenings, can be ignited with a lighted match and will burn briefly and without harming the plant. It has large, lemon-scented leaves, composed of six to twelve leaflets, and five-petalled, asymmetrical flowers, pinkish white or white in colour, and up to 2.5cm (1in) across. The pink flowers have purple veining. In flower, *Dictamnus* looks well with other early-summer-flowering perennials, such as *Geranium psilostemon* and the bearded irises. In autumn, the flower stems gradually dry off, and the dark green leaves turn yellowish green or yellow, making this plant a good foil for autumn-flowering daisies, such as *Helenium* and *Rudbeckia*.

Habit: clump-forming, erect
Height: up to 90cm (36in)
Spread: 60cm (24in)
Flowering season: early summer
Origin of species: southern Europe to western Himalayas, northern China and Korea.
Hardiness: fully hardy UK; Zone 3 US
Cultivation: it is best in full sun or light shade in a fertile but well-drained soil; it resents disturbance and, if left alone, is long lived. It can be divided in autumn or spring, although it will take time to re-establish.

ABOVE LEFT **On a hot summer's evening, these flowers give off a volatile oil which, if lit, will burn for a short time without damaging the flowers.**
LEFT **How different this plant looks in seed! If you bring the seedpods inside, they will explode when they dry out, and shed their seed.**

GLOBE THISTLE
Echinops ritro

The globe thistle earns a place because it combines elegant foliage with unusual, long-lasting flowers, which may repeat, and also can be cut and dried for indoor decoration. The leaves, on hairy white stems, are elliptic, divided, extremely prickly, and rough-textured; they are dark green above, and greyish white and softly-hairy beneath. In late summer, spherical flower heads, up to 4.5cm (1¾in) across, appear; they are composed of many florets, which are initially steely blue and bristly, but turn bright blue when they open, and fade to pale blue before setting seed.

Echinops ritro is a striking plant for planting at the back of the border; it also associates well with hardy chrysanthemums and other members of the daisy family. There is an excellent cultivar called 'Veitch's Blue', which has slightly darker blue flower heads and grows to 90cm (36in); this is also a useful plant for cutting. *E. bannaticus* 'Taplow Blue', with bright blue flower heads and grey-green leaves, is a good choice if a taller (1.5m/5ft) plant is required.

ABOVE LEFT **The foliage is striking and elegant, but very prickly.**
TOP RIGHT **The flower heads start steely blue, but turn bright blue as the florets open.**
LOWER RIGHT **The seedheads can be cut and dried for indoor decoration.**

Habit: clump-forming, erect
Height: up to 75cm (30in)
Spread: 45cm (18in)
Flowering season: late summer to autumn
Origin: Europe to central Asia
Hardiness: fully hardy UK; Zone 3 US
Cultivation: this is a plant for a sunny border in free-draining, even poor soil. It needs little care, except deadheading if a second flush of flowers is wanted. Propagation is by division in spring or autumn.

SEA HOLLY
Eryngium bourgatii

Eryngium bourgatii is one of the sea hollies, much prized by gardeners for their long-lasting and unusual flowers and foliage, and by flower arrangers for the excellent cutting qualities of the flowers and seedheads. Sea hollies are semi-evergreen perennials, and *Eryngium bourgatii* is one of the best and most widely available. It has very spiny, grey curly leaves, with silver-veined, more or less heart-shaped basal leaves. The sculpted flowers consist of thistle-like, rounded blue heads, up to 3cm (1¼in) across, with spiny, blue-silver, ruff-like bracts, 6cm (2in) long. They appear over a long period from mid- to late summer. The flowers are held on sturdy branching blue stems. The dried, gold-brown flower heads and leaves last well into the winter and look stunning when silvered by frost.

This sea holly associates particularly well with lemon-yellow hemerocallis, *Argyranthemum* 'Jamaica Primrose' and *Helictotrichon*, but generally is capable of fitting in anywhere. There is a fine cultivar with darker flowers called *E. bourgatii* 'Oxford Blue'.

Other excellent small sea hollies include *E. × tripartitum* (which has smaller, daintier heads) and *E. × zabelii*. There is also a well-known, free-seeding biennial, called *E. giganteum* (Miss Willmott's ghost). If they are to be dried, sea hollies are best cut just before the flowers have fully opened.

ABOVE LEFT **The prickly basal leaves of this sea holly (shown here in late spring) bear a resemblance to holly, hence the common name.**
ABOVE RIGHT **The terminal blue flower opens first, in early summer; it is followed by those of the side branches.**
OPPOSITE **The seedheads, captured in autumn; they will last well into winter.**

Habit: clump-forming
Height: 45cm (18in)
Spread: 30cm (12in)
Flowering season: mid- to late summer
Origin: Spain
Hardiness: fully hardy UK; Zone 5 US
Cultivation: grow in a free-draining but not too fertile soil, in full sun. Propagate by taking root cuttings in winter, or sow seed in a cold frame when ripe.

BARRENWORT
Epimedium
x *versicolor*
'Sulphureum'

The epimediums are an attractive, and easy, race of ground-covering plants. *E.* x *versicolor* 'Sulphureum', derived from a cross between *E. grandiflorum* and *E. pinnatum* subsp. *colchicum*, is one of the best, because it combines good leaf colour in spring and autumn with pretty flowers, which do not hide themselves beneath the leaves. The new leaves, in spring, begin a very pale green and quickly acquire deep red tones, which contrast sharply with the predominant yellows and acid-greens of the spring garden. The 2cm (¾in) flowers are held on 30cm (12in) stems above the leaves, and are pale yellow with long spurs, like very small columbine (*Aquilegia*) flowers. The leaves fade to green until the autumn, when they take on bronze tints. They consist of between five and nine heart-shaped leaflets, with spiny edges. There are two other good *E.* x *versicolor* cultivars: 'Cupreum', with copper-red flowers, and 'Neosulphureum', with very pale yellow flowers.

Habit: clump-forming, but gradually spreading to form a 'carpet'
Height: up to 30cm (12in)
Spread: 30cm
Flowering season: early spring
Origin: garden origin
Hardiness: hardy UK (though flowers may be frosted); Zone 5 US
Cultivation: *E.* x *versicolor* 'Sulphureum' is more tolerant of a range of growing conditions than some other epimediums, but it grows best in humus-rich, leafy soil in partial shade. Remove old leaves in late winter. Divide after flowering, or in autumn.

ABOVE LEFT **The leaves in autumn take on interesting tones. They persist through the winter, making this an excellent ground-covering plant, once established.**
LEFT **A striking combination of colours make this an exciting plant for the spring garden.**

SPURGE
Euphorbia griffithii 'Fireglow'

Spurges, or euphorbias, are very varied and useful garden plants. *E. griffithii* finds a place here because the emerging lance-shaped leaves are flushed red in spring, before turning to dark green with pink midribs, and then again to red and yellow tints in autumn. In early summer, flattish heads of orange-red to red flowers (strictly speaking, bracts surrounding the small yellow flowers) are borne on erect stems. Some excellent selections have been made, which are better than the species: for example 'Dixter', with particularly good flower and leaf colour, and a more compact habit; 'Fireglow', with bright orange-red bracts. Because *E. griffithii* has slowly creeping rhizomes, it can be a little invasive in some soils, but the cultivars are rather better behaved. All associate very well with ferns, such as *Matteuccia struthiopteris*, both visually and because they like the same conditions. All euphorbias exude a poisonous milky sap, when cut, which causes irritation if it comes into contact with skin or eyes.

ABOVE LEFT **The young leaves are flushed red in spring, before turning dark green with pink midribs, as here.**

ABOVE RIGHT **In early summer, this spurge is striking because of the orange-red bracts that surround tiny yellow flowers.**

Habit: erect, dense
Height: 90cm (36in)
Spread: 60cm (24in)
Flowering season: early summer
Origin of species: Bhutan, Tibet, and south-west China
Hardiness: fully hardy UK; Zone 6 US
Cultivation: this plant likes a moist soil in light shade. Pull up rhizomes if it becomes invasive. Propagation is by division in spring.

CRANESBILL
Geranium macrorrhizum

Cranesbills are among the most garden-worthy of hardy perennials: they make good groundcover and are also evergreen or semi-evergreen, so are particularly valuable. My favourite is the semi-evergreen *Geranium macrorrhizum*, because its leaves take on pretty tints in the colder months.

The leaves are large, up to 20cm (8in) across, seven-lobed, strongly aromatic, and light green. They turn bronze and red in autumn. The flowers are not very large, up to 2.5cm (1in) across, but quite profuse; they are magenta in colour, and have prominent red calyces, styles and stamens. The root is a rhizome, hence the name 'macrorrhizum'.

There is a white cultivar 'Album', which is choicer, as well as soft-pink 'Ingwersen's Variety', and 'Variegatum', which has grey-green leaves with a creamy variegation, and pink flowers.

Habit: clump-forming, ground-covering
Height: up to 50cm (20in)
Spread: up to 60cm (24in)
Flowering season: late spring to early summer
Origin: southern Europe
Hardiness: fully hardy UK; Zone 5 US
Cultivation: plant in any garden soil, preferably in sun or semi-shade, but will also tolerate shade. Cut back after flowering to encourage a second flush of flowers, and new leaves. Propagate by division in spring.

ABOVE LEFT **A very reliable ground-covering plant, with pleasing, sticky and aromatic leaves all through the season.**
LEFT **These leaves colour in autumn and winter but die off only gradually, as new ones replace them in spring.**

BLUE OAT GRASS
Helictotrichon sempervirens (syn. *Avena candida*)

The blue oat grass is a valuable plant for the garden with all-year-round appeal, for it is evergreen and always looks neat and tidy, even in winter. It is a naturally mound-making plant and is never invasive, unlike some of the other grasses. The leaves are flat, thin, silvery blue and very long, and the arching stems carry drooping, open panicles of straw-coloured, oat-like flowers in early and midsummer. The leaves and seedheads endure into the winter months, giving interest at a difficult time of year, and this plant looks very impressive on a frosty morning.

Blue oat grass makes a lovely foil for silver-leaved plants, whose planting conditions it tends to share, together with purple and pink flowers. It also makes a very good subject for a pot or urn, as it is resistant to drought, and the setting makes a feature of its impressive habit. A similar plant, though smaller in all its parts, is *Festuca glauca*.

ABOVE LEFT **In early and midsummer, arching stems of oat-like flowers erupt from a silver-blue clump.**
ABOVE RIGHT **The seedheads last well into winter. Being clump-forming, this grass is never invasive.**

Habit: tuft-forming, arching
Height: up to 1.2m (4ft)
Spread: 60cm (24in)
Flowering season: early and midsummer
Origin: central and south-west Europe
Hardiness: fully hardy UK; Zone 5 US
Cultivation: plant in spring in a preferably alkaline, well-drained, not especially fertile soil, in full sun. This plant will grow in gravel. Tidy the plant by removing the flowered stems in spring. Protect in winter in colder areas. Propagate by sowing seed, or dividing plants in spring

BEAR'S FOOT, STINKING HELLEBORE
Helleborus foetidus

Hellebores are well established as invaluable evergreen, or semi-evergreen, bone-hardy perennials for the winter garden. Flowers that come out in short days are a blessing, and one of the most reliable winter flowerers is the so-called 'bear's foot' or 'stinking hellebore' (*Helleborus foetidus*). The name 'bear's foot' refers to the rosette of finger-like leaves, which are divided into seven to ten narrow, toothed, dark green leaflets. The 'stinking hellebore' refers to the unpleasant odour of these leaves when crushed. The flowers are drooping and bell-shaped, and light lime-green with a thin purple-red rim. They are held on sturdy, bare stalks, up to 75cm (30in) high, above the leaves. This plant looks well with *Erica carnea* 'Golden Starlet'.

A superior cultivar is *Helleborus foetidus* 'Wester Flisk'. It has reddish brown stems and leaf stalks. Both the species and its cultivar flower from late winter to spring, and set seed freely ('Wester Flisk' comes true from seed). The other virtue of these plants, besides their flowering time, is that they will survive quite well in a dry, shaded site, although they perform better in a moister, richer soil. All hellebores are poisonous if eaten, and may irritate the skin if touched.

Habit: clump-forming, upright
Height: up to 75cm (30in)
Spread: 45cm (18in)
Flowering season: late winter and early spring
Origin: western and central Europe
Hardiness: fully hardy UK; Zone 5 US
Cultivation: this hellebore grows best in a sheltered place, in a well-drained but enriched soil, in sun or partial shade. It seeds freely, but not excessively. Sow seed when ripe.

ABOVE LEFT **Hellebores tolerate a range of growing conditions, even the dry, shaded soil found under a tree.**
LEFT **An early and reliable plant which flowers in late winter – for that alone, it deserves a place in the garden.**

YELLOW SKUNK CABBAGE
Lysichiton americanus

The yellow skunk cabbage is a most unfortunate name for this plant. Although it is indeed yellow, the smell, though musky, hardly deserves to be compared with that of a skunk, nor does the leaf particularly resemble that of a cabbage. Indeed, this is a most distinctive plant, popular with anyone lucky enough to have a bog or stream garden. It is related to *Arum*, and has strongly veined, shiny, pea-green, paddle-shaped leaves as much as 1.2m (4ft) long. These appear as the flowers are beginning to fade. The flower, like that of arums, is made up of an outer, fleshy, hood-like bract (spathe), which is keel-shaped and bright yellow, and partly encloses an inner flower spike (spadix). The singularity of this perennial, combined with the harmonious colours, make it an excellent companion for irises, primulas and other spring-flowering bog-lovers. There is a smaller, white-flowered lysichiton called *L. camtschatcensis*, which is sweetly scented and a better bet for a small water garden.

ABOVE LEFT **Slow to establish and come into flower, lysichitons are nevertheless almost indispensible in the bog garden.**
ABOVE RIGHT **The leaves do not appear until the flowers are fading. This plant has underground rhizomes, which stabilize it on stream banks but are not easy to divide.**

Habit: upright
Height: up to 1m (3ft)
Spread: 1.5m (5ft)
Flowering season: early spring
Origin: western North America
Hardiness: fully hardy UK; Zone 5 US
Cultivation: this plant needs a permanently moist soil, in full sun or partial shade. It can be propagated by division, but it is not an easy task with mature plants. Seed must be kept permanently wet if it is to germinate.

SHUTTLECOCK FERN
Matteuccia struthiopteris

Ferns are under-used in most gardens, but have the merit of thriving where many other types of plant do not. *Matteuccia struthiopteris*, often known as the 'shuttlecock fern', is so-called because, as they develop, the sterile fronds radiate upwards and outwards from the base, much like a shuttlecock. It is deciduous, and the deeply-cut, lance-shaped fronds unfurl like a bishop's crozier in spring. They are pale green, and grow up to 1.5m (5ft) long in good conditions. In late summer, shorter brown fertile fronds, up to 50cm (20in) long, grow inside the sterile ones. The sterile outer fronds turn brown and shaggier as the season wears on, and eventually disintegrate; however, the inner fertile ones last throughout the winter, and can look very fetching, especially when coated with rime. This fern is best planted in a large, shady border, waterside or semi-wild area, since it can be invasive.

ABOVE LEFT **This fern is a lovely and unusual sight in spring, when the sterile fronds gradually elongate and unfold.**
ABOVE RIGHT **The fertile fronds can just be glimpsed inside the 'shuttlecock' of the outer sterile ones.**
OPPOSITE **The outer fronds colour and become progressively shaggier before they disintegrate, leaving only the fertile ones to persist through the winter.**

Habit: upright
Height: up to 1.5m (5ft)
Spread: up to 1m (3ft)
Flowering season: late summer
Origin: Europe, North America, eastern Asia
Hardiness: fully hardy UK; Zone 2 US
Cultivation: this fern is best grown in a neutral or acid, fertile, moisture-retentive soil, in partial shade. It can be propagated by dividing the rhizomes in spring.

ZEBRA GRASS
Miscanthus sinensis 'Zebrinus'

Grasses and sedges add form and colour to the garden through most of the year, their colours changing subtly, but irrevocably, as the season draws on. Some of the most popular – perhaps because they are not as invasive as many other grasses – are the 'eulalias', that is, cultivars of *Miscanthus sinensis*. They grow up to 2.5m (8ft) high, so can add verticality to a border, without necessarily a corresponding breadth. The leaves are erect, but arch towards the ends, and are blue-green with a silver midrib. The silver-purple flowers are borne in dense, arching panicles at the end of the stems in early autumn.

Miscanthus sinensis 'Zebrinus', or zebra grass, is a well-known cultivar which develops horizontal bands on the leaves in midsummer; these are golden-yellow or deep creamy white in colour. It reaches only about 1.2 to 1.5m (4 to 5ft) high, but is a striking plant in the border and, like other cultivars, has foliage that turns yellow in autumn. For best effect, leave the stems uncut over winter, and cut them down in spring, as the new leaves begin to emerge.

ABOVE LEFT **The zebra grass makes an imposing foliage plant in the border throughout summer.**
ABOVE RIGHT **As the flowers appear, the leaves turn to russet brown or yellow, although the horizontal banding is still just visible.**

Habit: erect, arching
Height: up to 1.5m (5ft)
Spread: up to 1.2m (4ft)
Flowering season: early autumn
Origin of species: south-east Asia
Hardiness: fully hardy UK; Zone 5 US
Cultivation: *M. sinensis* and its cultivars thrive in a fertile, moist soil in full sun. Divide and pot up in spring, and grow on before planting out.

SHOO-FLY
Nicandra physalodes

Annual plants should not be discounted entirely, for some are capable of multiseasonal interest. One such is the hardy annual, *Nicandra physalodes*, otherwise known as the 'shoo-fly'. This easy-to-grow flower has branching stems, up to 90cm (36in) tall, and lance-shaped, mid-green leaves. Violet-blue, white-throated, bell-shaped flowers, 4cm (1½in) across, are borne from midsummer until early autumn. Each flower lasts for one day. The flowers quite quickly transmute into spherical, winged, papery green fruit, like round lanterns; these contain the brown berries. The fruit gives a pointer to one of the plant's other common names, 'apple of Peru', but it is in fact poisonous, and must not be eaten. It can, however, be cut and dried for indoor decoration. This plant is considered by some to deter the insect pest, whitefly.

Habit: upright, branching

Height: 90cm (36in)

Spread: 30cm (12in)

Flowering season: midsummer to autumn

Origin: Peru

Hardiness: hardy annual UK; hardy annual US

Cultivation: This is a plant of waste ground in Peru, so a well-drained, even poor soil, in full sun is ideal. Sow seed *in situ* in mid-spring. It sets seed quite freely.

ABOVE RIGHT **Small, violet-blue, bell-shaped flowers offer a charming display from midsummer to early autumn.**

RIGHT **A dramatic metamorphosis has taken place. Within a matter of weeks, the flowers have transformed into lantern-shaped fruit containing brown berries.**

CAUCASIAN PEONY
Paeonia mlokosewitschii

An ability to spell or pronounce the name of this plant is not a pre-requisite to growing it, thank goodness, for this is one of the finest of all peonies. Its charm lies partly in its very attractive, long-lasting foliage, which is an excellent foil for the flowers. The leaves are divided into nine ovate or obovate leaflets, smooth above and hairy beneath, which are often rounded at the apex. When they emerge in early spring, they are a warm red, but later turn blue-green, sometimes edged with red, and finally purple in autumn. The flowers, up to 12cm (5in) across, appear singly on naked stems above them in late spring; they are single, bowl-shaped, a lovely soft lemon-yellow, and are followed by conspicuous, lobed fruit, which splits to reveal the black seeds on a red background inside. The flowers of this herbaceous perennial are, admittedly, short lived, but the fruit and leaves make up for this, especially as the latter take on reddish tints in autumn, before falling.

Habit: erect, clump-forming
Height: 60cm (24in)
Spread: 60cm (24in)
Flowering season: late spring
Origin: Caucasus
Hardiness: fully hardy UK; Zone 5 US
Cultivation: this is a plant for a conspicuous place in the border, where it will flourish, if left undisturbed, for many years. It thrives in a deep, fertile but well-drained soil, in full sun. Propagation can be by seed if sown in autumn, although it is very slow, or by root cuttings in winter.

ABOVE LEFT **The leaves begin life a warm brownish red, then turn blue-green, and end the season with red and purple tints.**
LEFT **This peony has particularly beautiful, bowl-shaped, lemon-yellow flowers, which harmonize well with the blue-green leaves.**

OPIUM POPPY
Papaver somniferum

Many people consider this annual species, the so-called 'opium poppy', as a weed, because it seeds so freely and has rather fleshy leaves; however, in a big garden, it is a very ornamental border plant, producing flowers of the utmost delicacy in summer, and long-lasting capsule seedheads in autumn. The single, semi-double or double flowers are often pink, darkly blotched in the centre, but can be anything from white to mauve to yellow to deep purple. They burst out from small round buds, resembling the finest tissue paper. These are followed by the distinctive seed capsules, which are smooth, plump, grey-green in colour and are rounded but with flat tops. The leaves, also an attractive feature, are lobed with serrated edges, smooth, blue-grey and bloomy. There are a number of good cultivars, available as seed, including 'Paeony-Flowered' in a range of colour, and 'White Cloud'. There is also 'Hen and Chickens', which has single pink flowers and very large seedpods, surrounded by a brood of little ones.

Opium poppies are very useful for filling gaps in borders where pink, white and blue flowers predominate in late summer. These poppies will set seed very freely if allowed to do so. This can make an excellent effect, but it is important not simply to neglect them, particularly in smaller gardens where they can easily become invasive.

ABOVE LEFT **Opium poppies can be either single- or double-flowered, and come in a wide range of colours.**
ABOVE RIGHT **The seed capsules are much prized by flower arrangers because of their shape and sturdy stems, and because they can be easily dried.**

Habit: upright
Height: about 1m (3ft)
Spread: about 30cm (12in)
Flowering season: mid- to late summer
Origin: unknown
Hardiness: fully hardy UK; hardy annual US
Cultivation: sow seed *in situ* when the plants are to flower in spring in well-cultivated, fertile soil in full sun. If you don't want them to seed freely, cut the capsules on long stems, just before they are ripe, and use them for indoor decoration.

PASQUE FLOWER
Pulsatilla vulgaris (syn. *Anemone pulsatilla*)

The common name, pasque flower, celebrates the fact that the flower of this perennial usually comes out at about Easter time. Apart from the flowers, which resemble those of anemones (to which they are closely related), and appealing foliage, pulsatillas are well known for their beautiful seedheads, not unlike those of clematis species (to which they are also related).

Pulsatilla vulgaris makes a low mound of pretty, fern-like, finely divided, silky-hairy foliage. In spring, hairy stems grow up to 25cm (10in), carrying single, purple, six-petalled, bell-shaped flowers, with conspicuous bosses of yellow stamens within. They are followed by silky seedheads. The leaves gradually lose their hairs, so appear less silvery as the season wears on. This is a plant for the sunny rock garden or raised bed, but it will also survive in a well-drained border. Cultivars include 'Alba', with white flowers; and 'Röde Klokke' (syn. 'Red Clock', 'Rote Glocke') and var. *rubra*, in red.

ABOVE LEFT **Silky soft, young foliage accompanies gentle purple flowers in spring.**
ABOVE RIGHT **By early summer, the flower heads have turned to silken seedheads, which catch the light easily.**

Habit: clump-forming
Height: about 25cm (10in)
Spread: about 20cm (8in)
Flowering season: spring
Origin: Britain, Europe, Scandinavia
Hardiness: fully hardy UK; Zone 5 US
Cultivation: this is a plant for cold climates, for it tends to die out in mild areas. It likes a free-draining, gritty, alkaline soil in full sun. Take root cuttings in winter, or sow seed in pots when ripe.

COMMON RUE
Ruta graveolens

The common rue is a plant often consigned to herb gardens, but it is an excellent denizen of a prominent sunny border, because of its most attractive evergreen foliage, which is set off well by yellow flowers in summer.

Rue is a neat, rounded sub-shrub with a woody base. The pungent leaves are ovate, deeply cut and many lobed, and are smooth and deep blue-green. In midsummer, yellow four-petalled flowers are borne above the leaves in flattish cymes. The best cultivar is the widely available 'Jackman's Blue', which has deeper blue-green foliage and a more compact habit, but flowers less freely. It is important to realize that rue is not a culinary herb; in fact, all parts are poisonous and the foliage can cause a skin rash if touched, so it is advisable to plant and prune using gloves. Plant it among silver-leaved plants, or use it as small, trimmed specimens in pots.

Habit: compact, rounded
Height: up to 75cm (30in)
Spread: 75cm (30in)
Flowering season: summer
Origin: southern Europe
Hardiness: fully hardy UK; Zone 5 US
Cultivation: grow in a well-drained, even poor, alkaline soil, preferably in full sun. A place in gravel is ideal, as it will stand considerable heat. Trim over in spring to keep a neat, compact plant. Propagate by semi-ripe cuttings in summer.

ABOVE RIGHT **The combination of lime-yellow flowers and blue-green foliage is a winning one in 'Jackman's Blue'.**
RIGHT **The foliage is evergreen, so deserves a prominent place in a sunny spot.**

COMMON SAGE
Salvia officinalis

This is the common sage, a vital inhabitant of the herb garden, but also an attractive ornamental border plant. It is an evergreen, sub-shrubby perennial. The leaves are oval, grey-green, and woolly in texture. They are highly fragrant, especially when crushed. In summer, lilac-blue flowers are borne at the end of the stems, or in the leaf axils. There are a number of fine coloured-leaved cultivars, such as 'Icterina' (green with yellow and gold);

'Purpurascens' (purple, especially the younger leaves); and 'Tricolor' (purple, pink and white). These are not as vigorous or as hardy as the species, but are excellent in a well-drained soil, or container, in a very sunny spot, where they associate well with other Mediterranean-type plants, such as rue (*Ruta*) and artemisias. In the purple cultivar, the young leaves are darker in colour than the mature ones, which creates an interesting effect.

ABOVE LEFT **The common sage is reasonably hardy, especially when grown in a well-drained soil, and will survive some frost.**
ABOVE RIGHT **The contrast of lilac-blue flowers with the felty grey-green leaves is a highly attractive one.**

Habit: mound-forming, shrubby
Height: 75cm (30in)
Spread: 75cm (30in)
Flowering season: early to midsummer
Origin: Mediterranean region
Hardiness: frost hardy UK; Zone 5 US
Cultivation: this plant needs a very well-drained soil, in a sunny place, to thrive; otherwise winter wet may kill it. Trim over in early spring to keep the plant neat and young. The younger it remains, the more likely it will withstand bad weather. It is not long lived, but can be easily propagated by taking softwood cuttings in early summer.

ICE PLANT
Sedum 'Herbstfreude'

The sedum is a most amenable garden perennial, the smaller ones often found in rockeries, while the larger cultivars are honoured members of the mixed border. It is not always appreciated, however, what good value they give, particularly if their seedheads are left uncut in autumn. Indeed, 'Herbstfreude' (syn. 'Autumn Joy'), is the ideal multiseasonal plant, for it never loses its coherence. It becomes a substantial clump-forming plant, up to 60cm (24in) tall when flowering, with succulent, glaucous-green stems with large, obovate, toothed, bluish green leaves at the base. In early autumn, 20cm (8in) flat heads of buds appear, pale green at first, but then opening to small, star-shaped pink flowers. As time wears on, these darken to bronze- or copper-red. The seedheads will endure, gradually darkening to deep brown, while the stems become straw-yellow. A clump in early winter, rimed with sparkling frost, is a lovely sight.

Habit: clump-forming, erect
Height: up to 60cm (24in)
Spread: up to 60cm (24in)
Flowering season: early autumn
Origin: garden origin
Hardiness: fully hardy UK; Zone 4 US
Cultivation: 'Herbstfreude' is happy in sun or partial shade, and will grow in a well-drained reasonably fertile soil. It can be left alone for several years, without division, but in time the stems will get overcrowded. Deadhead in early spring, as the new growth begins. Take softwood cuttings in summer.

ABOVE RIGHT **The fresh green leaves appear early in spring, and are an excellent foil to more colourful summer flowers.**
RIGHT **The flowers are a great draw for butterflies; they gradually darken in colour before setting seed.**

HOUSELEEK
Sempervivum tectorum 'Atropurpureum'

The common name for this perennial is houseleek, because of the tradition of growing sempervivums on roofs, thanks to their ability to sustain drought and poor soil. They form neat, evergreen, symmetrical, succulent rosettes, up to 15cm (6in) across, which are composed of small, obovate, bristle-tipped, tough leaves. In the cultivar 'Atropurpureum', the leaves are suffused with deep red and purple tones. In summer, the flower stems emerge from the rosettes; they have hairy leaves all the way up, and the pink flowers are held in flattened heads, 10cm (4in) across. The rosettes die after flowering, but are replaced by new offsets. Houseleeks are good plants for containers or a rock garden.

Habit: rosette-forming
Height: about 15cm (6in)
Spread: 30cm (12in), but indefinite clumps
Flowering season: summer
Origin of species: southern Europe
Hardiness: fully hardy UK; Zone 5 US
Cultivation: grow in poor, well-drained soil, in a sunny position. If the soil is too moisture-retentive, add grit. Propagate by digging up and replanting the rooted offsets in spring or early summer.

ABOVE LEFT The sempervivum rosettes spread by offsets to form sizeable clumps. They always remain neat and fresh.
LEFT The flowers are held in flattened heads, made up of dozens of dusty pink, star-shaped flowers.

LAMB'S EARS
Stachys byzantina 'Cotton Boll' (syn. 'Sheila McQueen')

This is a cultivar of the well-known perennial *Stachys byzantina* (lamb's ears) which has such distinctive, intensely furry silver leaves. It makes a good ground-covering plant for a sunny place and associates particularly well with other coloured-leaved plants, and also shrub roses. It is evergreen, or 'ever-grey' (although it can look a bit tatty in the winter), with elliptic or lance-shaped, toothed, deeply veined leaves covered with dense silvery hairs. The flower stems are up to 45cm (18in) tall, but the flowers do not appear; instead they are encased in silver-white bobbles, like cotton wool balls, in the summer. Other good cultivars are 'Big Ears', with large leaves; 'Primrose Heron', which has lemon-silver leaves; and 'Silver Carpet', with intensely silver, greyish white leaves but no flowers. The species *Stachys byzantina* does produce woolly, pale purple flowers, but it is not a neat plant when it is flowering.

ABOVE LEFT **The intensely furry, ever-grey lamb's ear leaves are irresistible to children.**
ABOVE RIGHT **Unusual flowers, encased in silver-white bobbles, appear in summer.**

Habit: mat-forming
Height: 45cm (18in)
Spread: 45–60cm (18–24in)
Flowering season: summer to early autumn
Origin of species: Asia minor
Hardiness: fully hardy UK; Zone 5 US
Cultivation: lamb's ears are happiest in a free-draining soil in full sun. They will withstand drought. In spring, they can be divided, or rooted sections severed, and replanted.

TREES

*Trees give a garden a sense of permanence and maturity and, if chosen carefully,
they will reward the onlooker throughout the year. They provide interest with
their bark and habit in winter, flowers in spring and summer, foliage
all through the season, and fruit and leaf colour in autumn.*

BELOW **An unusual tree, *Prunus subhirtella* 'Autumnalis', flowers off and on
through the winter, after these brightly-coloured leaves have dropped.**

SNAKE-BARK MAPLE
Acer capillipes

The snake-bark maples are a group of small trees, distinguished by the extraordinary latitudinal streaking on their barks, which resembles snake skin, to the fanciful at least. These are ideal trees for anyone who wants multiseasonal effects, for they have fine winter skeletons, attractive leaves, shoots, and seeds, and lovely autumn colour.

Acer capillipes is one of the finest snake-bark maples. The streaking on its bark is silvery green when mature and reddish green when young, while the leaf shoots are a glistening red. The shiny green leaves are broadly ovate, but with three lobes, which have marked points to them; they turn red or orange in autumn. The flowers are not very showy, but the clusters of green-yellow winged seeds are appealing. This is a tree to use as a specimen in a lawn or border, preferably where the light will catch its bark, but it is best planted in a sheltered place, where frost will not damage the bark in spring. Other excellent snake-barks include *Acer davidii*, larger and with yellow flowers; *A. d.* 'Ernest Wilson', with bright orange autumn foliage; and *Acer pensylvanicum* with clear yellow leaves in autumn.

Habit: dense, arching, spreading
Height: about 6m (20ft)
Spread: about 3m (10ft)
Flowering season: spring
Origin: Japan
Hardiness: fully hardy UK; Zone 5 US
Cultivation: plant in sun or semi-shade in any reasonably fertile garden soil, preferably in a sheltered place. Pruning is not necessary except for shaping and should be done in late autumn. Propagation can be by seed sown in trays left outside in autumn, or this plant can be grafted in late winter

ABOVE LEFT **A portion of trunk showing clearly how this tree received its common name of the snake-bark maple.**
ABOVE RIGHT **The pendent, greenish white flowers are just setting seed.**
RIGHT **The red and orange autumn colour is reliable in this species.**

PAPER-BARK MAPLE
Acer griseum

To my mind, this is one of the finest of all small deciduous trees. Its distinction lies mainly in the rusty brown bark, which peels freely, in tatters, revealing cinnamon-orange new bark beneath. This peeling occurs particularly on the trunk and on older branches, so a mature tree is a very fine sight. The shape is upright, then spreading, which makes this tree a good choice for a small garden – perhaps where there is room for only one or two trees – especially as it is slow growing.

The leaves are made up of three dark green, ovate, toothed leaflets; they colour very well in the autumn, exhibiting yellow, orange, scarlet and crimson tints. The flowers are small, yellow and pendent, and are followed by hairy, winged fruit. However, the seed rarely germinates, which means that *Acer griseum* is a fairly expensive tree to buy.

Habit: upright, spreading
Height: up to 10m (30ft)
Spread: up to 3m (10ft)
Flowering season: spring
Origin: China
Hardiness: fully hardy UK; zone 5 US
Cultivation: *Acer griseum* is one of the least fussy of the maples; it will even grow on chalk. but it is best in neutral, fertile, moist but well-drained soil. It is best grown in light shade. If required, prune when the plant first becomes dormant in late autumn. Propagation is by grafting in winter.

TOP LEFT *Acer griseum* **makes a handsome tree, even for a small garden.**
BELOW LEFT **This tree can be relied upon to produce scarlet autumn colour, which contrasts well with the mahogany bark.**
BELOW RIGHT **A close-up of the trunk, showing how the outer layers peel in tatters, revealing a smooth cinnamon-orange bark**

JAPANESE MAPLE
Acer palmatum 'Sango-kaku' (syn. 'Senkaki')

'Sango-kaku' means 'coral tower' in Japanese, and is an apt name for a small tree or very large shrub, with an upright habit and wonderful bright coral-red branches in winter. The best colour is to be found on the youngest stems. The branches lose something of their brilliant colour in summer, but the leaves are attractive enough in their own right for this not to matter. These are small and shaped like a hand, and are yellow, tinged with pink, then soon fresh bright green, and turn a pretty yellow before they fall in late autumn. *Acer palmatum* 'Sango-kaku' (also grown under its synonym, 'Senkaki'), makes an excellent specimen in a lawn or large border.

Habit: upright
Height: up to 7m (22ft)
Spread: up to 3m (10ft)
Flowering season: spring
Origin of species: Japan
Hardiness: fully hardy UK; Zone 6 US
Cultivation: this plant will grow in most soils, but it must never be allowed to waterlog or dry out in summer. As with other cultivars of *Acer palmatum*, this plant should be placed where it is sheltered from wind, and from spring frosts. In very cold sites, mulch around the roots in autumn. Some judicious pruning to promote young growth is worthwhile. Propagation is by grafting in winter.

TOP RIGHT **The bright coral-red branches come to prominence after the leaves have fallen in the autumn.**
BELOW LEFT **The young leaves in spring combine well with the red stems.**
BELOW RIGHT **The leaves turn a complex mix of colours in the autumn.**

SERVICEBERRY, SNOWY MESPILUS
Amelanchier lamarckii

The serviceberry, or snowy mespilus, is a very attractive small tree or multi-stemmed shrub, which produces many hanging clusters of small, pure-white, single, star-shaped flowers, at the same time as bronze young leaves, in spring. The flowers are followed by round, purple-black fruit, and the oval, finely toothed 8cm (3in) leaves turn from dark green in summer to striking shades of orange and red in autumn. The berries are not very conspicuous. Nevertheless, if you have only room for one small tree in your garden, this is an excellent candidate for the position. Even better though, if you have a sufficiently large garden, is to associate this tree with other choice small trees or shrubs, which can match the amelanchier for gorgeous autumn colour, such as *Cornus* 'Eddie's White Wonder', or one of the *Acer palmatum* cultivars.

ABOVE LEFT **The impact of the flowers is enhanced by the presence of the very young, coppery brown leaves.**
ABOVE RIGHT **The leaves of amelanchiers colour best if the tree is grown in an acid soil.**

Habit: rounded, spreading
Height: up to 10m (30ft)
Spread: up to 10m (30ft)
Flowering season: mid-spring
Origin: possibly North America; naturalized in Europe
Hardiness: fully hardy UK; Zone 4 US
Cultivation: *Amelanchier lamarckii* likes a soil that is neither waterlogged nor very dry, preferably neutral or acid. A sheltered position in full sun or light shade is ideal. Thin out the branches of multi-stemmed shrubs when they become overcrowded. Propagation is by seed, when ripe, or semi-ripe cuttings in summer.

MADRONO
Arbutus menziesii

For all-year-round interest, no plant can better *Arbutus menziesii*. Its combination of evergreen leaves, peeling bark, and long-lasting flowers and fruit ensure it a place amongst the immortals. That said, it will never be every gardener's choice, for it is slow growing and fussy about soil and aspect.

The so-called madrono has a broadly spreading habit, often with several trunks growing vertically, or near-vertically, close to ground level. The distinctive bark is reddish brown on the outside, revealing green beneath, as papery strips of bark peel off. The evergreen leaves are oval, glossy and dark green on the upper side, and bluish white beneath. In late spring, urn-shaped white flowers, up to 8mm (⅜in) long, appear profusely, in upright panicles, up to 20cm (8in) long. These are often followed by orange-red, warty, 1cm (½in) round, long-lasting fruit, which takes many months to ripen. This is a tree principally for a woodland garden, or as a specimen in the lawn or border.

There are some other fine *Arbutus* trees, such as *Arbutus* x *andrachnoides* and *A. unedo* (the latter of which has two excellent compact cultivars, 'Compacta' and 'Elfin King'), which have the advantage of growing on alkaline soil. All prefer a cool climate, without extremes of temperature.

ABOVE LEFT **The panicles of white flowers in late spring and early summer transform the look of this tree.**
ABOVE RIGHT **The strawberry-like fruit takes many months to ripen completely.**

Habit: round, spreading
Height: up to 15m (50ft)
Spread: up to 10m (30ft)
Flowering season: late spring, early summer
Origin: western North America
Hardiness: fully hardy UK; Zone 7 US
Cultivation: grow this plant in a sheltered, sunny place in a fertile, moist but free-draining acid soil. Plant young trees as the roots resent disturbance. Do not prune unless really necessary and then in winter. Take cuttings in late summer, or sow seed when ripe.

CANOE BIRCH, PAPER BIRCH
Betula papyrifera

Betula papyrifera, known as the canoe birch (because the bark was used by native Americans to make canoes) or paper birch (because of its paper-like bark), is a medium-sized, conical-shaped tree, with bright white bark, containing lots of obvious pores. It peels in thin layers, exposing the orange-brown trunk beneath. The hanging male catkins are yellow, and up to 10cm (4in) long; the female ones are green and shorter. Both male and female catkins are carried in very early spring. The leaves are ovate, dark green, toothed, and turn to yellow and yellow-orange before they fall. A small group or grove of these trees is a wonderful sight, and is the way they grow in the wild. One of the great virtues of birches, for the owner of a small garden, is that they have a very open habit, so rarely cast much shade. Another is that they grow quickly initially, but never make huge trees. They are worth placing carefully, with a dark background to show up the trunk.

Other excellent barked birches are *Betula alleghaniensis*, with peeling yellow-brown bark and yellow-green leaves; *B. albosinensis* var. *septentrionalis*, with pale orange-red bark; *B. ermanii*, with pinkish cream bark; and *B. utilis* var. *jacquemontii* (of which 'Silver Shadow' and 'Jermyns' are excellent cultivars), with copper-brown or pinkish bark.

ABOVE LEFT **This is a splendid and trouble-free specimen tree for any garden.**
ABOVE RIGHT **The autumn leaf colour is reliable and, as the leaves fall, the white trunk and stems are revealed.**

Habit: conical, open
Height: up to 18m (60ft)
Spread: 5m (15ft)
Flowering season: early spring
Origin: North America
Hardiness: fully hardy UK; Zone 6 US
Cultivation: this birch will grow well in most soils, except shallow chalk ones, but does best in a deep, reasonably fertile, moist but well-drained soil, in sun or light shade. If necessary for shape, prune in early winter. Propagate by taking softwood cuttings in summer or by grafting in winter

COCKSPUR HAWTHORN
Crataegus persimilis '*Prunifolia*'

This is a small, deciduous tree of distinctive habit, with wide-spreading branches, some of which may droop enough to reach the ground. A member of the hawthorn family, it is well armed with long, sharp spines, but despite that, is distinguished enough in flower, fruit and autumn colour to be worthy of a place in every garden. The flowers have a heavy scent: they are white, with pink anthers, and borne in round, dense clusters in early summer. These are followed by rounded 'haws', or berries, which begin green and gradually become rich red before they fall in late autumn. The leaves are small, broadly oval, toothed, and bright dark green in summer, but turn to brilliant shades of scarlet and crimson in autumn.

Also worth growing for the same attributes is *C.* x *lavallei* 'Carrierei'.

Habit: rounded, spreading, often of greater width than height
Height: up to 8m (25ft)
Spread: up to 10m (30ft)
Flowering season: early summer
Origin of species: probably North America
Hardiness: fully hardy UK; Zone 6 US
Cultivation: this plant will grow in any reasonable garden soil, in full sun. It is tolerant of industrial pollution, and will grow in coastal gardens. Pruning is usually unnecessary.

TOP **A mature tree in autumn is an awe-inspiring sight, for the leaves turn to brilliant shades of scarlet and crimson.**
ABOVE LEFT **The tree is generously covered in dense clusters of white, strongly fragrant flowers in early summer.**
ABOVE RIGHT **The scarlet 'haws', or berries, are set off well by the bright dark green leaves before they change colour.**

TULIP TREE
Liriodendron tulipifera

This is a tree for a place of honour in a large garden, as it can grow to 30m (100ft) or more in time, especially in mild areas. It can make a magnificent addition to a garden with its unique, large, deciduous leaves and showy flowers. The leaves are broad, with two side lobes and two lobes at the tips; they are dark green in summer, turning a pretty butter-yellow in autumn. The 7cm (3in) flowers – which are cup-shaped like tulips (hence the common name), green in colour, with orange basal bands and protruding stamens – are carried in early summer; they are often masked somewhat by the dense foliage. The flowers are followed by conical fruits. The tree does not flower until it has reached at least 15 years old. Mature trees possess an interesting silvery grey and fissured bark. There is also a yellow-variegated cultivar, *L. tulipifera* 'Aureomarginatum', which is less vigorous.

Habit: broadly conical
Height: up to 30m (100ft)
Spread: 10–15m (30–50ft), although usually less in the UK
Flowering season: early to midsummer
Origin: eastern North America
Hardiness: fully hardy UK, but grows best in mild areas; Zone 5 US
Cultivation: to thrive, tulip trees need a fertile, slightly acid soil, in full sun or partial shade. Plant them from a container because they have brittle roots that are easily damaged. Pruning is usually unnecessary. Sow seed in autumn, or graft in spring.

TOP **This is a tree to grow in a prominent position, because of its handsome habit. It can grow to 30m (100ft) tall in time.**
BELOW LEFT **These unusual flowers appear in early summer. Although often obscured by foliage, and not obvious from a distance, they are well worth searching for.**
BELOW RIGHT **The leaves of the tulip tree are unique in shape, bearing little resemblance to those of any other tree, except the related Chinese tulip tree (*Liriodendron chinense*).**

DOMESTIC APPLE
Malus 'Worcester Pearmain'

Although the domestic, cultivated apple tree is one of the most beautiful denizens of the garden, it is often underrated as an ornamental tree. Yet not only is its fruitfulness in autumn captivating, but the blossom in late spring is sublime. The white, cup-shaped flowers open from charming, fat pink buds, and last for a fortnight or more, depending on the weather. Different cultivated varieties flower at slightly different times, so it is possible to have apple blossom in the garden for up to six weeks. The habit of old apple trees, especially those not grown on dwarfing rootstocks, is also very attractive, and is perfectly suited to

a country or 'cottage' garden. The weight of fruit in the autumn often bears down the branches, thus changing the aspect of the tree from upright and spreading to positively rounded.

'Worcester Pearmain' flowers mid-season, at the same time as 'Cox's Orange Pippin'. Its fruits are round, and in colour a sumptuous red on a yellow-green ground, with some russet spots. The flesh inside is white, juicy and very sweet, making it a dessert rather than a cooking variety. This apple is picked in very early autumn and, as it does not keep well, should be eaten immediately. It is usually a heavy cropper.

ABOVE LEFT **This apple's flowers are distinctive, being pink at first and fading to silvery white. They appear in late spring.**
ABOVE RIGHT **'Worcester Pearmain' apples show just how ornamental a domestic fruit tree can be in early autumn.**

Habit: spreading
Height: depends on rootstock
Spread: depends on rootstock
Flowering season: late spring
Origin: garden origin
Hardiness: fully hardy UK; Zone 5 US
Cultivation: apples need to be planted in a fertile, well-drained but moisture-retentive soil, preferably slightly on the acid side. An organic mulch in spring is advisable. Pruning is necessary, especially in the early years. Pests and diseases can be troublesome. Propagate by grafting in winter.

TEA CRAB APPLE
Malus hupehensis

Although rather too vigorous for the very small garden, this is a marvellous deciduous tree for all seasons, where there is space for it to spread. It makes a handsome, rounded and spreading shape, with upswept branches. Its great glory, however, is the profusion of pink-budded, white, scented, cup-shaped flowers in late spring; these are held on long stalks so that the flowers extend beyond the leaves, adding greatly to the attraction of the overall picture. The flowers are followed by masses of small, glossy red fruit in autumn. The leaves are dark green and oval, and take on autumn tints before they fall. In the winter, the bark, which is brown and fissured into rectangular plates, can be seen to advantage. The common name refers to the fact that a tea is made from the leaves in the tree's native China.

TOP The spreading nature of this tree adds greatly to its appeal, although it does mean that it is not suitable for a small garden.
LEFT The pretty and delicate white flowers are profusely borne on long stalks in late spring.
BELOW LEFT Once the fruits have set, they gradually increase in size and then turn from green to glossy red.

Habit: rounded and spreading
Height: up to 12m (40ft)
Spread: up to 12m (40ft)
Flowering season: late spring
Origin: China
Hardiness: fully hardy UK; Zone 5 US
Cultivation: grows in any reasonably fertile soil, in full sun or light shade. Pruning minimal. This tree can be propagated by seed, which should be sown in a seedbed in the autumn, or in a tray left outside over the winter.

CRAB APPLE
Malus × *zumi* 'Golden Hornet'

This is one of the showiest ornamental crab apple cultivars there is. Like most members of the *Rosaceae* family, it can offer both very attractive flowers in spring, and showy fruits in late summer and autumn. It is a modest, rounded, deciduous tree, ideal for small gardens. The flowers are 4cm (1½in) across, pink in bud, and pinkish white when open. The leaves are small, bright green, narrowly oval, and toothed. The fruit is round, 2.5cm (1in) across, and borne in hanging clusters of three or four; it is green initially, then turns to butter-yellow. It persists long after the leaves have fallen, and is the tree's most striking feature.

Malus 'Butterball' is similar to *M.* × *zumi* 'Golden Hornet', and there are a number of other small, garden-worthy *Malus* cultivars, such as 'Liset', with dark purple-pink flowers and cherry-like fruit; 'Red Jade', with white or pink-flushed flowers and bright red fruit; 'Red Sentinel', with white flowers and yellow-flushed red fruit; and 'Royalty', with crimson-purple flowers and dark red fruit. Ornamental crab apples associate well with each other, or with cultivated fruit trees in a mixed orchard.

ABOVE LEFT **The flowers in spring give no hint as to the size and colour of the autumn fruits. Nevertheless, they make a lovely picture.**

ABOVE RIGHT **This tree almost completely changes its aspect in half a year. The fruit turns gradually from green to a gorgeous, warm butter-yellow.**

Habit: rounded
Height: up to 5m (15ft)
Spread: up to 4m (12ft)
Flowering season: late spring
Origin: garden origin
Hardiness: fully hardy UK; Zone 5 US
Cultivation: grow in any reasonably fertile and well-drained soil, in full sun or light shade. Propagate by grafting in winter, or bud in late summer.

MEDLAR
Mespilus germanica

Mespilus germanica, or medlar, is that invaluable garden asset – a highly ornamental fruit tree. This duality of purpose makes it a winner for smaller gardens, yet it is not widely planted, perhaps because the fruit it produces is rather an acquired taste! It is deciduous, and makes an interesting, wide-spreading, rounded shape, and has grey-brown bark, which cracks with age. The shoots are often thorny. The leaves are large, up to 15cm (6in) long by 5cm (2in) wide, hairy, oblong and dark green, and acquire yellow and brown tints in autumn. The single, unscented flowers are also large, up to 5cm (2in) across, white, and borne from late spring to early summer, and occasionally again in late summer. They are followed by unique fruits, which are brown, rough-textured, spherical except for flattened tops, and with persistent, long, tapering calyces. The fruit is picked in mid-autumn and left to soften enough to eat. It is quite acid, however, and is therefore best made into a jam or jelly, rather than eaten raw. 'Nottingham' is a commonly planted cultivar.

ABOVE LEFT **The white flowers of the medlar are very large for a fruit tree.**
ABOVE RIGHT **The fruit is not edible until it has started to rot and become soft. Even then, it has an acidic flavour.**

Habit: round-headed, spreading
Height: up to 6m (20ft)
Spread: 5m (15ft) or more
Flowering season: late spring to early summer, sometimes again in late summer
Origin: south-east Europe, south-west Asia
Hardiness: fully hardy UK; Zone 6 US
Cultivation: grow in a sheltered place in a well-drained, but not too dry soil in sun or dappled shade. It needs little pruning. Sow seed in a seedbed when ripe.

FUJI CHERRY
Prunus incisa

One of the most charming of early-flowering ornamental cherries is *Prunus incisa*, the so-called 'Fuji cherry'. The flowers appear before the leaves in early spring; they are produced in profusion, either alone or in small clusters, and are single, saucer-shaped, and either white or pale pink in colour. They are occasionally followed by small, ovoid, deep purple fruit. The green leaves are ovate and toothed, up to 6cm (2½in) long; they are bronze when they emerge and, in autumn, turn lovely flame tints before they fall.

Prunus incisa may be grown either as a large, spreading shrub or a small, rounded tree, which makes it suitable for smaller gardens. It can even be trimmed to make a hedge, and has long been a popular subject for bonsai treatment. It associates well with early-flowering narcissi and other bulbs. There are a number of named cultivars available, such as 'February Pink', with pale pink flowers in winter and early spring; 'Kojo-no-mai', with pale red flowers; 'Oshidori'; and 'Praecox', which has pink buds that open to white flowers in late winter.

Habit: spreading, rounded
Height: about 6m (20ft)
Spread: about 5–6m (16–20ft)
Flowering season: early spring
Origin: Japan
Hardiness: fully hardy UK; Zone 6 US
Cultivation: plant in well-drained but moisture-retentive, even alkaline, soil. Full sun is best for flowering and autumn colour. Pruning minimal. Propagate by sowing seed in a cold frame in early spring.

ABOVE RIGHT **One of the earliest ornamental cherry trees to flower, its boughs are laden with blossom in early spring.**
RIGHT **The magnificent autumn display of leaves more than compensates for the usually small yield of fruit.**

Prunus subhirtella 'Autumnalis'

The charming pinkish white, semi-double flowers of this deciduous ornamental cherry are produced at any time between late autumn and mid-spring, in mild weather, and in sufficient quantity usually to make an impact. The biggest flushes come as the leaves fall, and again in early spring. They are 2cm (¾in) across, and borne in small clusters of up to five flowers. This tree does fruit, having small, nearly-black cherries, but they are not conspicuous or profuse. The tree is medium-sized, and spreading with a round head. The leaves are 8cm (3in)

long, oval and tapered, and toothed; they have a bronze tinge to them when young, and turn yellow and orange in autumn before falling. There is also a pink cultivar, *P. s.* 'Autumnalis Rosea'.

ABOVE LEFT **The flowers look especially lovely in late winter and early spring.**
ABOVE RIGHT **The autumn colour of the leaves is usually yellow or orange. As the leaves fall, the first flowers are ready to open.**
LEFT **A close-up of the flowers.**

Habit: broad, spreading
Height: up to 8m (25ft)
Spread: up to 8m (25ft)
Flowering season: autumn to spring
Origin of species: Japan
Hardiness: fully hardy UK; Zone 6 US
Cultivation: plant in full sun for best flowers and autumn colour, in moist but well-drained soil. Avoid planting in a lawn because of the shallowness of the roots. Pruning is not often necessary, but can be done in midsummer, if required. Commercial plants are grafted.

WILLOW-LEAVED PEAR
Pyrus salicifolia 'Pendula'

The willow-leaved pear is a deservedly popular, small deciduous tree to grow as a specimen in a lawn or next to a pond. The strongly pendulous, dense, stiff branches more-or-less hide the tree's trunk, and can reach ground level. The thin, willow-like leaves are white and densely hairy in spring, making a good foil for the dense clusters of creamy white pear blossom. The flowers are followed by small, brown, pear-like fruits, which are inedible. *Pyrus nivalis*, the snow pear, also has silvery leaves, but a strictly upright habit.

Habit: strongly pendulous, curving tips
Height: up to 6m (20ft)
Spread: up to 4m (12ft)
Flowering season: mid-spring
Origin of species: south-east Europe, Turkey
Hardiness: fully hardy UK; Zone 5 US
Cultivation: this tree grows best in a fertile, heavy soil, in sun or partial shade, but is quite tolerant of both drought and excess moisture, as well as air pollution. It can be pruned lightly to shape in summer. It is commercially budded or grafted.

TOP **Creamy white clusters of pear-like flowers adorn this tree in mid-spring.**
ABOVE RIGHT **The weeping habit of this tree is clearly visible in the dormant season.**
RIGHT **The densely hairy spring leaves lose their feltiness as the season progresses.**

Sorbus commixta 'Embley'

Often known as *Sorbus discolor*, this is another fine small to medium-sized tree, giving good shape, attractive flowers and excellent autumn leaf and berry colour. 'Embley' is the cultivar most usually seen in gardens. It has large, showy clusters of white flowers in late spring, followed by masses of orange-red berries. The leaves are 15cm (6in) long with up to 17 lance-shaped, tapering, serrated, dark green leaflets. These turn from green to purple and then rich, glowing red in autumn; they stay on the tree well into autumn. 'Embley' makes a splendid specimen tree, or looks good in a glade of similar, or identical, trees.

ABOVE LEFT *Sorbus commixta* 'Embley' makes a very fine mature tree, and tolerates most soil types.
ABOVE RIGHT This sorbus exhibits marvellous and very reliable, long-lasting autumn colour.

Habit: broadly conical
Height: up to 10m (30ft)
Spread: up to 7m (22ft)
Flowering season: late spring
Origin of species: Japan, Korea
Hardiness: fully hardy UK; Zone 6 US
Cultivation: 'Embley' will grow in any well-drained soil in sun or light shade.

KASHMIR MOUNTAIN ASH
Sorbus cashmiriana

Sorbus cashmiriana is one of the most ornamental of all the rowans or mountain ashes, because of its particularly striking bunches of flowers and its long-lasting berries. The habit of this deciduous tree is open and spreading. The deep green leaves are grey-green beneath and 15cm (6in) long; they are divided into between 17 and 19 lance-shaped leaflets, and are deeply toothed. They turn yellow in autumn. The flowers are borne in 12cm (5in) clusters in late spring, and are a very soft, pale pink. The berries that follow are bright white, tinged with pink at first, and hang from red stalks in loose clusters; each one is 12mm (½in) across. They are profusely carried, and are left on the tree long after the leaves have fallen to create an attractive display.

ABOVE LEFT **The charming, pale pink flowers of *Sorbus cashmiriana* are carried in clusters, opening in late spring.**

ABOVE RIGHT **Masses of round white berries, initially flushed pink, hang in loose clusters from red stalks over a long period.**

Habit: rounded, spreading
Height: up to 7m (22ft)
Spread: up to 8m (25ft)
Flowering season: late spring
Origin: western Himalaya
Hardiness: fully hardy UK; Zone 6 US
Cultivation: sorbuses will grow in any well-drained soil in sun or light shade, but are happiest where the soil is acid or neutral. They can withstand some drought. It is possible to sow the seed outside in a tray in autumn although, commercially, these trees are budded or grafted.

glossary

This glossary is intended to give the meaning of technical terms used in the book, in case they cause confusion or puzzlement. I have also included the meanings of a number of botanical Latin words, which describe 'species', and appear in the book, especially in the section 'Plants for All Seasons'. This list is not comprehensive for I have translated names (as they appear) which are descriptive, but not those which refer to, for example, the discoverer of a plant or where it comes from. Thus I have translated *alba*, but not *bourgatii*, on the grounds that the first is used for identification, while the second is not.

Acid Refers to a soil with a pH lower than neutral (7).
alatus Winged.
alba White.
Alkaline Refers to soil with a pH higher than neutral (7).
Annual A plant that completes its life-cycle within one growing season.
Anther Part of the stamen bearing pollen.
aquifolium Pointed leaves.
autumnalis Of the autumn.
Bulb Storage organ, consisting of underground bud and scale leaves.
caerulea Blue.
Calyx (pl. calyces) The group of sepals which enclose a flower bud.
Capsule Dry envelope containing seeds.
cardunculus Thistle-like.
carnea Flesh-coloured.
Catkin Stalkless flowers, without petals, either male or female; in case of *Betula*, drooping.
Chlorophyll Green pigment in leaves.
Clone A group of plants derived from a single individual by vegetative propagation, therefore identical.
Cordate Heart-shaped (of leaves).
Corm Storage organ; a swollen underground stem (e.g. crocus).
Corolla Collective name for petals in a flowerhead
Cultivar A 'cultivated variety', which, unlike a species, has been raised in cultivation.

Cutting The general word for a section of stem, leaf or root which is used for propagation. 'Softwood', 'semi-ripe', and 'hardwood' are types of cuttings, depending on the time of year when the cutting is taken.
Cyme Flat or round-topped, branching flower head. The central flowers are the first to open.
Deadhead Cut off dead flower or seed-heads.
Deciduous Losing foliage annually, usually in autumn.
Division A method of propagation consisting of splitting a plant's roots into at least two and replanting separately.
Dormancy A period of inactivity, for example, the period for bulbs between the leaves dying down and the new shoots growing.
Elliptic Egg-shaped, applied usually to leaf shape.
Ericaceous An adjective applied to plants of the *Ericaceae* family, e.g. *Rhododendron*.
Evergreen Retaining foliage throughout the year.
Fastigate A form of growth with erect branches, e.g. certain forms of trees.
Floret A tiny, individual flower, part of a dense flower head (as in grass and daisy families).
foetidus Stinking.
Frost tender Prone to damage in temperatures below 5C (41F).
Garden origin In this case, a term used to distinguish a plant bred, or selected, rather than collected in the wild.
Genus (pl. genera) A group of related plants, below 'family' and above 'species'.
Grafting A technique of propagation when the rootstock of one plant is united and grows together with the scion (shoot) of another.
graveolens Strong-smelling.
Hardy (or Fully hardy) A term applied to plants which can withstand very low temperatures. 'Frost hardy' plants can survive a few degrees of frost.
hederifolium With leaves like an ivy.
Herbaceous perennial A non-woody plant that survives for several years,

dying down in the winter but shooting again in spring.
horizontalis Growing horizontally.
incisa With deeply cut (leaf) margins.
inodorum Without scent.
intermedia Intermediate (between two parent plants).
Internode The area of stem between the leaf joints.
Invasive Used to describe plants that are so vigorous in growth that they overwhelm other plants.
lacteus Milk-coloured.
Lanceolate Lancehead shaped.
Lateral Sideshoot.
Layering A technique of propagation involving the pegging of a shoot to the ground, until roots form at the point of contact.
Leaflet A division of a compound leaf.
Leaf axil The angle between a leaf stalk and a shoot.
Linear Long and narrow with parallel margins, e.g. grass leaf.
Lobe Usually rounded segment of a leaf, cut to halfway or less from the centre of the leaf.
luteum Yellow.
macropetala With large petals.
macrorrhizum With large roots.
major Greater.
mas Male.
Mulch A topdressing used to preserve moisture, suppress weeds and, in winter, protect plants from the cold.
Node Place on stem where leaf or sideshoot arises.
Obovate More-or-less oval leaf, but broadest furthest from the leaf-stalk.
Offset A small new plant that arises, attached, to one side of an established plant, e.g. sempervivum, and many bulbs.
Opposite A term used for those leaves which arise in pairs, rather than alternately, e.g. *Acer*.
Ovate A leaf which is more or less oval, but a little wider towards the base.
Ovoid An egg-shaped object, e.g. some berries.
palmatum Hand-like.
Panicle A branched raceme (*see below*).

papyifera Papery.

peltata Shield-like.

pendula Drooping.

Perennial A non-woody plant which survives for several years, dying down in the winter but shooting again in spring.

petiolaris Long-petioled.

Petiole leaf-stalk.

Pinnate Describes a compound leaf, where leaflets arise, either opposite or alternately, on each side of a central axis.

plicatum Pleated.

Pollarding The technique of cutting a tree back hard to its main trunk annually, in order to produce a quantity of young shoots, e.g. willow, or to restrict its growth, e.g. *Catalpa*.

procumbens Lying flat.

pseaudocamellia Like a false camellia.

purpurea Purple.

quercifolia With leaves like an oak.

Raceme A flower head of stalked flowers arising from an unbranched main shoot.

The flowers tend to open from the bottom up.

Rootstock The lower part of a woody plant, on to which is grafted a scion, e.g. apple trees. Rootstocks affect the vigour of the tree.

rubiginosa Rust-coloured.

rugosa Wrinkled.

salicifolia With leaves like a willow.

sanguinea Blood-red.

Scion A shoot which is grafted onto the rootstock of a related plant, and gives the new plant its genetic characteristics.

sempervirens Evergreen.

Serrate The name given to a toothed leaf margin, with the teeth facing forwards.

somniferum Sleep-inducing.

Spadix A fleshy flower-spike in the *Arum* family.

Spathe A hood-like bract enclosing a spadix in the *Arum* family.

Stamen Male part of flower.

Stooling The lower part of a woody plant, on to which is grafted a scion, e.g. apple trees. Rootstocks affect the vigour of the tree.

sulphureum Pale yellow.

superba Magnificent.

Toothed Refers to a leaf which has shallow serrations to the margin.

Tuber Underground storage organ of swollen root or stem.

tulipfera With flowers like a tulip.

Umbel A flat- or round-topped flowerhead, where individual flowers spring from a common place.

Variegation Refers to a leaf, usually exhibiting more than one colour.

Venation Pattern of veining in a leaf or flower.

versicolour Changeable in colour.

vinifera Wine-producing.

vitellina Orange-yellow.

vulgaris Common.

zebrinus Striped.

further reading

A book of this kind is impossible to write without reference, from time to time, to selected parts of the vast body of modern horticultural and botanical literature. Much of this literature is available to general readers, in libraries and/or in bookshops. The following is a short selection of books which I have found particularly useful and I hope readers will find useful too, if they wish to expand their knowledge of plants for all seasons.

The RHS Plant Finder, ed. Tony Lord (published annually) (Dorling Kindersley, 1998)

The Royal Horticultural Society A–Z Encyclopedia of Garden Plants, ed. Christopher Brickell (Dorling Kindersley, 1996)

Botanica: The Illustrated A–Z of Over 10,000 Garden Plants and How to Plant Them (Mynah, 1997)

Reader's Digest New Encyclopedia of Garden Plants and Flowers (Reader's Digest, 1997)

The Royal Horticultural Society Dictionary of Gardening (4 volumes) (Clarendon Press, 1951)

The New Royal Horticultural Society Dictionary of Gardening, ed. Anthony Huxley, etc. (Macmillan, 1992)

The Gardener's Dictionary of Horticultural Terms, Harold Bagust (Cassell, 1992)

Trees and Shrubs Hardy in the British Isles, W.J. Bean (John Murray, 8th edition, 1970–88)

The Hillier Gardener's Guide to Trees and Shrubs (David and Charles, 1995)

The Gardener's Illustrated Encyclopedia of Climbers and Wall Shrubs, Brian Davis (Viking, 1990)

Shrubs, Martin Rix and Roger Phillips (Pan Books, 1989)

Perennial Garden Plants, Graham Stuart Thomas (Dent, 1990)

Hardy Perennials, Graham Rice (Penguin, 1997)

Perennials and Their Garden Habitats, Hansen and Stahl (Cambridge University Press, 1993)

Perennials, Martyn Rix and Roger Phillips (2 volumes) (Pan Books, 1993)

Bulbs, Martyn Rix and Roger Phillips (Pan Books, 1989)

Performance Plants: 150 Best Plants for Your Garden, Andrew Lawson (Frances Lincoln, 1992)

Christopher Brickell's Garden Plants, (Pavilion, 1995)

index

acknowledgments

All the following photography is by Howard Rice, who with the publishers wishes to give grateful thanks to the gardens and garden-owners listed below:

t = top, b = bottom, c = centre, l = left, r = right

Beth Chatto Gardens, Elmstead Market, Essex: 41b, 106 121; Cambridge Garden Plants, Horningsea: 9 t, 10t, 16, 45, 46r, 92, 97, 97, 112; Cambridge University Botanic Garden: Front cover bl, Front cover br, Back cover bl, Back cover br, 1, 2, 3, 6–7, 9b, 10b, 11, 17l, 18, 20, 21, 22b, 23t, 23, 25, 30, 31, 32t, 32b, 34, 35r, 39, 41t, 44, 48, 49l, 50, 51, 52, 53, 53 56, 60, 61, 62, 63, 71, 73, 75, 77, 79, 80, 82, 83r, 91, 95, 98, 100, 101, 102, 103, 105, 110, 111, 118, 122, 123, 124t, 124br, 127l, 128, 129, 132c, 134l, 135, 139; Clare College, Cambridge: Back cover t, 26b, 55,

96, 113; Coton Orchards, Madingley, Cambridge: 131l; David Austin Roses, Wolverhampton: 29t, 72t; Denmans Garden, W. Sussex: 8; East Bergholt Place Garden, Suffolk: 57, 133, 138; Sally & Don Edwards: 94; Emmanuel College, Cambridge: 134r; Mr & Mrs Hawkins: 88; Hergest Croft Garden, Hereford & Worcs: 40b; Hopleys Plants, Much Hadham, Herts: 137tr, 137b; Hyde Hall Garden, Essex: 24, 38, 68, 70, 74, 78, 116, 132t, 132b, 137tl; Joy Larkcom: 89r; Meredith Lloyd-Evans 87; Madingley Hall, Cambridge: 22t, 27, 42–43, 84, 99, 104, 117, 120; Monksilver Nursery, Cottenham, Cambridge: 17r, 90; John Morley: 89l; Paradise Centre, Lamarsh: 83l; Julia Procopé: 114b; Mr & Mrs Rice: Front cover t, 15, 64, 65, 66, 67, 115, 125bl, 125br, 136; Robinson College, Cambridge: 14, 107; The Royal Horticultural Society's Garden, Wisley: 4–5, 12–13, 26t, 28, 35l, 36, 36, 37, 40t, 47, 54, 58, 59,

69, 76r, 86, 119, 131r; Saville Gardens, Surrey: Front cover tl, Front cover tR, 19l, 32c, 33, 76l, 93, 109, 125t; Scotsdales Nursey & Garden Centre, Cambridge: 126; Mr & Mrs C. Sprigg: 108; Josie & Mervyn Stuart-Smith: 46l, 114t; Wyken Hall, Suffolk: 19r; The American Cemetary, Cambridge: 29b, 72b, 130.

The publishers would also like to thank the following photographers for their kind permission to reproduce the following pictures: Eric Crichton: 85t, 85b; Garden Picture Library/Mark Bolton 124bl; Nadia Mackenzie: Back jacket flap l; Clive Nichols Garden Pictures: 49r; Fiona Rice: Back jacket flap r; Harry Smith Collection: 127r.

The publishers also wish to thank Polly Boyd for her editorial help.